THE PERSON AND WORK
OF THE
HOLY SPIRIT

Translated by J. D. Emerson
Vennes-sur Lausanne

RENÉ PACHE
THE PERSON AND WORK OF THE HOLY SPIRIT

MOODY PRESS
CHICAGO

© 1954 by
THE MOODY BIBLE INSTITUTE
OF CHICAGO

ISBN: 0-8024-6471-8

Moody Paperback Edition, 1979

27 28 Printing/AF/Year 93 92 91 90

Printed in the United States of America

INTRODUCTION

THE SUBJECT of the Holy Spirit is of extreme importance. We all need His presence and His power, and without Him it would be utterly impossible for us to live the Christian life and serve God.

Therefore, let us ask the Lord to guide us in our study by the same Spirit about whom we shall speak, and to renew our inner life and our testimony through the truths which He will reveal to us.

Let us approach this subject without fear. The many passages referring to it in Scripture prove to us that the Bible teaching concerning the Holy Spirit is both definite and complete. If we hold strictly to what is written, and to all that is written, we shall be kept from many a danger. My earnest prayer is that throughout the following pages we may simply let the Bible speak. If we succeed, it will not fail to enlighten and edify us. I do not wish, on any point, to impose on the reader my own interpretation of Scripture. I am fallible, and I strongly recommend the readers to enter the school of the only Teacher who leads into all truth. If some question appears to be insufficiently elucidated, turn again prayerfully to all the passages referring to it in the Bible. God will certainly fulfill His promise and give you, besides the light which you need, a personal conviction.

I apologize that certain chapters, especially the one on the receiving of the Spirit, contain inevitable repetitions. I have been obliged to deal with certain essential texts on various occasions and from different points of view in order to draw from them the many lessons which they contain. My aim has been in this way to render the exposition clearer and more complete.

The touchstone of all doctrine concerning the Holy Spirit is the following question: What place does it give to the Lord Jesus Christ? For the very role of the Spirit is to glorify the Saviour (John 16:14). Therefore let us not fear that our study will lead us no longer to give to Christ the place and the honor due to Him. On the contrary, if we allow ourselves to be led by God, this study will but exalt the only One who died and was raised up for us.

CONTENTS

Introduction

PART I
WHO IS THE SPIRIT?

PART II
THE WORK OF THE HOLY SPIRIT
BEFORE PENTECOST

PART III
THE WORK OF THE HOLY SPIRIT IN THE
HEART OF MAN SINCE PENTECOST

PART I
WHO IS THE SPIRIT?

The Revised Version (English) has been used throughout the book, with a few exceptions where Weymouth's *New Testament in Modern Speech* or a marginal reading of the Revised Version has been used.

CHAPTER 1

THE PERSONALITY OF THE HOLY SPIRIT

WHO IS THE HOLY SPIRIT? If we consider only Acts 1:8, "Ye shall receive power, after that the Holy Spirit is come upon you," we might think that the Spirit is merely a power, strength coming from God, a blessing which He grants us. However, it is easy to demonstrate that the Holy Spirit is more than this. He is a person.

I. THE HOLY SPIRIT ACTS AS A PERSON

Let us note some of the actions which are attributed to Him and cannot be the expression of a power or of a thing.

1. He dwells in believers (John 14:17)
2. He teaches; He brings to remembrance (John 14:26)
3. He testifies (John 15:26)
4. He convicts of sin (John 16:8)
5. He guides into all truth; He hears, He speaks, He shows (John 16:13)
6. He inspires Scripture and speaks through it (Acts 1: 16; II Peter 1:21)
7. He spoke to Philip (Acts 8:29)
8. He calls to the ministry (Acts 13:2)
9. He sends forth His servants (Acts 13:4)
10. He forbids certain actions (Acts 16:6, 7)
11. He intercedes, etc. (Rom. 8:26)

II. HE POSSESSES THE ESSENTIAL ATTRIBUTES OF PERSONALITY

The Spirit is endued with

1. A will. He bestows His gifts upon every man as He will (I Cor. 12:11)

2. Thought. God knows what is the mind of the Spirit (Rom. 8:27)

3. Knowledge. The Spirit knows and searches the things of God (I Cor. 2:10, 11)

4. Language. "We speak, not in words which man's wisdom teacheth, but which the Spirit teacheth, comparing spiritual things with spiritual" (I Cor. 2:13)

5. Love. Paul exhorts the Romans for the love of the Spirit, to strive together with him in their prayers (Rom. 15:30)

6. Goodness. "Thou gavest . . . thy good Spirit to instruct them" (Neh. 9:20)

III. THE NAMES WHICH ARE GIVEN HIM REVEAL BOTH HIS PERSONALITY AND HIS DIVINITY

1. He is called
   a. My Spirit (Gen. 6:3)
   b. The Spirit of God (II Chron. 15:1)
   c. The Spirit of the Lord (Isa. 11:2)
   d. The breath of the Almighty (Job 32:8)
   e. The Spirit of the Lord God (Isa. 61:1)
   f. The Spirit of your Father (Matt. 10:20)
   g. The Spirit of (Acts 16:7, A.S.V.)
   h. The Spirit of Christ (Rom. 8:9)
   i. The Spirit of His Son (Gal. 4:6)

Since the three divine Persons are one, it is not surprising that the Holy Spirit should receive without distinction one or the other of these appellations.

2. His other names completely demonstrate His qualities He is the Spirit
   a. Of holiness—the Holy Spirit (Psa. 51:11; Rom. 1:4)
   b. Of wisdom (Isa. 11:2)
   c. Of counsel (Isa. 11:2)
   d. Of understanding (Isa. 11:2)

    e. Of supplications (Zech. 12:10)
    f. Of worship (John 4:23)
    g. Of truth (John 14:17)
    h. Of comfort (John 14:26—the Comforter)
    i. Of life (Rom. 8:2)
    j. Of adoption (Rom. 8:15)
    k. Of faith (II Cor. 4:13)
    l. Of love (II Tim. 1:7)
    m. Of might (II Tim. 1:7)
    n. Of sound judgment (II Tim. 1:7, Weymouth)
    o. Of revelation (Eph. 1:17)
    p. Of power (Eph. 3:20; Rom. 15:13—the power of the Holy Ghost)
    q. Of eternity—the eternal Spirit (Heb. 9:14)
    r. Of grace (Heb. 10:29)
    s. Of glory (I Peter 4:14)

IV. THE SPIRIT CAN BE TREATED LIKE A PERSON

He can be
1. Lied to (Acts 5:3)
2. Tempted (Acts 5:9)
3. Resisted (Acts 7:51)
4. Grieved (Eph. 4:30)
5. Outraged (Heb. 10:29)
6. Blasphemed against (Matt. 12:31)
7. Called upon (Ezek. 37:9)

V. IN SPEAKING OF THE HOLY SPIRIT, JESUS USES THE MASCULINE, NOT THE NEUTER PRONOUN

In the original Greek text, the neuter word *Spirit* should be followed by the neuter pronoun. However, contrary to grammatical rules, the pronoun is masculine (e.g., John 16:7, 8, 13, 14, etc.) to emphasize the fact that the Holy Spirit is a person and not a thing.

CHAPTER 2

THE DIVINITY OF THE HOLY SPIRIT

THE SCRIPTURES do not limit themselves in emphasizing the personality of the Holy Spirit; at the same time, they affirm His divinity in a most positive way.

I. THE SPIRIT BEARS DIVINE NAMES

When He is called "the Spirit of God," that means that He is the very Person of God. I Corinthians 2:11 clearly shows that as man and his spirit make one and the same being, so God and His Spirit are only one: "For who among men knoweth the things of a man save the spirit of the man which is in him? Even so, the things of God none knoweth, save the Spirit of God."

II. THE SPIRIT POSSESSES DIVINE ATTRIBUTES

1. Omniscience. "The Spirit searcheth all things, yea, the deep things of God" (I Cor. 2:10, 11).

2. Omnipresence. "Whither shall I go from thy Spirit?" (Psa. 139:7). The Spirit dwells at the same time in the hearts of all believers (see John 14:17).

3. Omnipotence. "Not by might nor by power, but by my Spirit . . ." (Zech. 4:6). It is in fact the Spirit which creates. "The Spirit of God hath made me" (Job 33:4); "Thou sendest forth thy Spirit, they are created" (Psa. 104:30).

4. The Truth. Jesus can say, "I am the truth" because He is God. In the same manner, in I John 5:6, the Spirit is declared to be the Truth.

5. Unsearchable greatness. "Who hath directed the Spirit

of the Lord, or being his counselor hath taught him?" (Isa. 40:13).

Many other divine qualities are attributed to the Spirit by the very names that He bears.

6. He is the Spirit of life (Rom. 8:2) as God is the living God.

7. He is the Spirit of love (II Tim. 1:7) as God is love.

8. He is the Spirit of sound judgment (II Tim. 1:7, Weymouth) as God alone is wise (Rom. 16:27, etc.).

III. THE SPIRIT IS THE THIRD PERSON OF THE TRINITY

First of all, let us underline the fact that the Spirit is associated with the Father and the Son, and placed on the same level as They are (Matt. 28:19); the disciples must baptize in the name of the Father, of the Son and of the Holy Spirit, as the blessing is given by all three (II Cor. 13:14).

On the other hand, Jesus calls the Spirit "another" Comforter, thus referring to Him as to another Self (John 14:16). It is with the same meaning that He declares to His disciples that it is expedient for them to lose His bodily presence and to receive the Spirit in themselves (John 16:7). According to Romans 8:9-10, to receive the Spirit is to have Christ dwelling in us.

The unity between the three divine Persons is so great that Paul can declare with equal truth:

"Your body is a temple of the Holy Ghost which is in you" (I Cor. 6:19).

"Ye are a temple of God" (I Cor. 3:16).

"Christ in you" (Col. 1:27).

Indeed, God is indivisible, and it is impossible either to conceive of, or to receive one of the three Persons of the Trinity without the other two. This unity in plurality is incomprehensible to many people, and even becomes a pretext for unbelief. However, we must not forget that man himself is formed of three elements, the intimate union of which forms his personality: spirit, soul, and body (I Thess. 5:23). That which appears to be admissible with regard to man is far more so concerning the Deity. The latter is also one, although composed of three elements.

The unity of the three Persons of the Trinity does not prevent Them from each playing a particular part. The Father is greater than all (John 10:29). The Son does only what He sees the Father doing and fulfills His will (John 5:19, 30). The Holy Spirit is sent by the Father and by the Son (John 14:26 and 16:7); He is given in answer to the prayer of the Son and in His name; and His role is to glorify the Son by putting His presence in the hearts of His disciples (John 14:16, 26 and 16:14).

On the other hand, the unity between the Son and the Spirit is marked by the fact that the attitude adopted by men toward the one determines that which they maintain toward the other: he who rejects Christ resists the Holy Spirit; the one who accepts the Saviour receives the Holy Spirit; he who yields entirely to Jesus is used by the Holy Spirit.

IV. THE HOLY SPIRIT IS GOD HIMSELF

In summarizing, we can affirm the essential divinity of the Holy Spirit. Moreover, this truth is clearly proclaimed in the following texts:

The Lord is the Spirit (II Cor. 3:17).

God is a Spirit (John 4:24).

To lie to the Holy Spirit is to lie to God Himself (Acts 5:3, 4).

Other passages in the New Testament attribute directly to the Spirit words or acts which, in the Old, were attributed to God.

1. "Moses said unto them [the people], . . . Wherefore do ye tempt the Lord? . . . And he called the name of the place Massah and Meribah, . . . because they tempted the Lord" (Exod. 17:2-7). "Even as the Holy Ghost saith, Today if ye

hear His voice, harden not your hearts, as in the provocation
... wherewith your fathers tempted me by proving me" (Heb.
3:7-9).

2. "I heard the voice of the Lord saying, ... Go, and tell
this people: Hear ye indeed, but understand not" (Isa. 6:8-10).
"Well spake the Holy Ghost by Isaiah the prophet unto your
fathers, saying: Go thou unto this people, and say ..." (Acts
28:25-27).

3. The Lord said, "This is the covenant that I will make
with the house of Israel after those days, saith the Lord; I will
put my law in their inward parts ..." (Jer. 31:31-34). "And
the Holy Ghost also beareth witness to us: for after he hath
said, This is the covenant that I will make with them ..."
(Heb. 10:15-17).

The Spirit is therefore undeniably God Himself. In conclusion, let us examine two accessory points.

V. IS THERE ANY DIFFERENCE BETWEEN THE SPIRIT OF GOD AND THE SPIRIT OF THE GLORIFIED JESUS?

Some people say: When one believes, he receives the spirit
of Jesus (I John 4:2; Rom. 8:9); when he is baptized with
the Spirit, he receives the Holy Ghost. Can this be true? Are
there two Spirits?

No, there is one divine Spirit, the Holy Spirit; He is at the
same time the Spirit of the Father and of the Son, since they
are one. Moreover, since the Father and the Son are God, the
Spirit of the one or the other must equally be God.

It is for this reason that the Bible repeatedly states that there
is only one Spirit.

"There is ... one Spirit" (Eph. 4:4).

"We both have our access in one Spirit unto the Father"
(Eph. 2:18).

"All these worketh the one and the same Spirit ... in one

Spirit were we all baptized into one body" (I Cor. 12:11, 13).

The following passages testify clearly to this one Spirit, and at the same time give Him different names:

"Having been forbidden of the Holy Ghost to speak the word . . . they assayed to go into Bithynia; and the Spirit of Jesus suffered them not" (Acts 16:6, 7).

"If so be that the Spirit of God dwelleth in you. But if any man hath not the Spirit of Christ, he is none of his" (Rom. 8:9).

"For as many as are led by the Spirit of God, these are sons of God . . . Ye received the Spirit of adoption, whereby we cry, Abba, Father" (Rom. 8:14).

"But he that is joined unto the Lord is one spirit [the spirit of Christ] . . . Your body is the temple of the Holy Ghost" (I Cor. 6:17-19).

Therefore, what was stated above proves to be exact: in the Scriptures, the Holy Spirit, the Spirit of God and the Spirit of Christ are one and the same Person. In this connection, it is striking to note that in the same manner the Bible refers without distinction to the Gospel of God and the Gospel of Christ.

"Separated unto the gospel of God" (Rom. 1:1).

"God . . . whom I serve in my spirit in the gospel of his son" (Rom. 1:9).

"Ministering the gospel of God" (Rom. 15:16).

"I have fully preached the gospel of Christ" (Rom. 15:19).

Further mention is made of the grace of God (Gal. 2:21; 4:6) and the grace of Christ (Gal. 1:6; 6:18). And yet, nobody would think of saying that these are two kinds of Gospel or two kinds of grace.

VI. IF THERE IS ONLY ONE SPIRIT, WHY DOES REVELATION (1:4; 3:1; 4:5 AND 5:6) SPEAK OF "THE SEVEN SPIRITS OF GOD"?

Considering all these passages which demonstrate the unity

of the Spirit, this expression cannot mean that there are seven different ones. In order to understand it, let us remember that the Revelation often uses symbolical language. In this language, the number seven constantly signifies fullness and perfection (as already seen in the Old Testament). In Revelation 5:6 the Lamb slain has seven horns and seven eyes which are the seven spirits of God; this is an allusion to the perfect power and knowledge imparted to Him by the Spirit which He possesses without measure (John 3:34). The fact that the Holy Spirit in His perfect fullness remains one is further proved by Revelation 1:4-5: grace and peace are given to the churches from God, from the seven spirits which are before His throne, and from Jesus Christ, just as the blessing is given in the name of the Father, of the Son and of the Holy Ghost, for example in II Corinthians 13:14. It is therefore evident that there is one Spirit, and that this Spirit is God.

CONCLUSION

We have just seen that the Holy Spirit is a Person and the third Person of the divine Trinity.

The establishment of this fact is what gives a deep interest to the study which we are about to make on His work in the human heart. Indeed, if the Spirit were merely a power coming from above, it would be at my disposal and I could use it at will. But if the Spirit is a Person, and more than that, if He is God Himself, it is I who should be at His disposal, and love and obey Him in all things. Besides, receiving into our hearts not only a blessing, but the presence of the Almighty God is to have within us the source of all grace and of all possibility. Let us beware of failing to recognize the true nature of the Holy Spirit.

CHAPTER 3

THE SYMBOLS OF THE HOLY SPIRIT

THE HOLY SCRIPTURES use the following symbols to represent the Spirit and to help us to understand better either His person or His work.

I. THE BREATH OR THE WIND (in the original language, the word "spirit" also means "breath")

According to Genesis 2:7 God breathed upon Adam a breath of life in the same manner as later on He will give to "the new man" the breath of the Spirit. We read in Job 32:8: "But there is a spirit in man, and the inspiration of the Almighty giveth them understanding," and in Job 33:4: "The Spirit of God has made me, and the breath of the Almighty giveth me life."

Ezekiel prophesies and says: "Come from the four winds, O breath, and breathe upon these slain, that they may live" (37:9). Jesus Himself, speaking of the regenerative work of the Spirit, says, "The wind bloweth where it listeth, and thou hearest the sound thereof, but knowest not whence it cometh, and whither it goeth" (John 3:8). Then, when He sends forth His disciples, He breathes upon them saying, "Receive ye the Holy Ghost" (John 20:22). Finally, when the Spirit Himself descends on the day of Pentecost, He is accompanied by a sound as of a rushing mighty wind, which fills all the house where the disciples are sitting (Acts 2:2).

What does this symbol mean? The above passages allow us to think that he stresses the impetuous, invisible and unexpected action of the Spirit; it shows also that this action is

20

heavenly, that it comes from above, that it is sovereign and infinitely above man. Finally, if the Spirit is called the Breath of the Almighty, it is because He is His direct emanation, the manifestation of His very presence.

Since we are speaking of the impetuous action of the Spirit, the following passages are of interest, as they will illustrate it in a special manner: "And the Spirit lifted me up between the earth and the heaven, and brought me in the visions of God to Jerusalem . . . The Spirit lifted me up, and brought me unto the east gate . . . And the Spirit of the Lord fell upon me, and he said unto me . . ." (Ezek. 8:3; 11:1, 5). "The Spirit of the Lord caught away Philip . . . [who] was found at Azotus . . ." (Acts 8:39-40). In these different cases, does not the Spirit seem to act as a sudden and mighty wind, which seizes an object and makes of it that which He desires?

II. THE DOVE

While Jesus was being baptized by John the Baptist, "the Holy Ghost descended in a bodily shape as a dove upon him" (Luke 3:22).

Some people think that the dove set free by Noah, when he was in the ark (Gen. 8:8-12), is also an image of the Holy Spirit. On the sin-laden and devastated earth, the Spirit, as He cannot find a pure place wherein to dwell, comes back and rests upon Christ, represented by the Ark of salvation. Then, the Spirit takes the Church away from the earth (draws it up into the heavens) as the first fruit of humanity in the same way that the dove brought back an olive branch in her beak. Then when the time is fully come, the Spirit will be able to spread over all the earth which, during the Millennium, will be effectively filled with the knowledge of God, as the waters cover the sea. The raven which is an unclean bird feeding upon dead bodies, is an image of the flesh which delights itself in the midst of all impurities.

Why does the Scripture use this image? Without a doubt it

is to remind us that, like the dove, the Holy Spirit is characterized by gentleness, tenderness and purity. He not only possesses irresistible power, He is also a Spirit of love, grace, consolation and innocence.

III. OIL

The New Testament speaks constantly of the "unction" of the Holy Spirit. Jesus attributes to Himself the word of Isaiah: "The Spirit of the Lord is upon me, because he has anointed me" (Luke 4:18). Peter says in Acts 10:38: "God hath anointed Jesus of Nazareth with the Holy Spirit and with power." The Epistle to Hebrews adds, "Therefore God, even thy God hath anointed thee with the oil of gladness" (1:9). Finally, Paul and John declare, "Now he . . . who hath anointed us, is God" (II Cor. 1:21). "But ye have an unction from the Holy One, and ye know all things" (I John 2:20).

All these passages are allusions to the unction of oil described in the Old Testament for priests, prophets and kings. The Holy Spirit therefore applies the indispensable preparation for the ministry (Acts 1:8).

On the other hand, it seems that the oil which the wise virgins carefully put into their lamps (Matt. 25:4) also represents the Spirit without whom no one belongs to Christ (Rom. 8:9). In the Old Testament the holy oil alone continually lighted the temple, where God was worshiped and where the person and the work of Christ were wholly symbolized (Exod. 27:20-21). In the same manner, the Spirit illuminates and glorifies Christ before our eyes; He gives us understanding of heavenly truths, and enables us to worship in spirit and in truth (John 16:14; I John 2:27; Phil. 3:3).

According to Leviticus 14:17 and 8:30, the oil was put over the blood to sanctify the lepers and the priests. In the same manner we, as sinners called to serve the living God, are sanctified by the blood of the cross and by the power of the Spirit (Rom. 8:2-3). Finally there is a beautiful illustration of the source, constant renewal and light of the divine "oil" in Zechariah 4:2-5, the conclusion, "Not by might, nor by power, but by my Spirit, saith the Lord of hosts" in verse 6.

IV. THE FIRE

On the day of Pentecost, tongues resembling tongues of fire rested upon each of the disciples, and they were all filled with the Holy Spirit (Acts 2:3-4). Twice John the Baptist in speaking of Jesus said: "He will baptize you with the Holy Ghost and with fire; whose fan is in his hand, and he will throughly purge his floor and gather his wheat into the garner; but he will burn up the chaff with unquenchable fire" (Matt. 3:11-12; Luke 3:16-17).

The fire, according to the constant use made of it by the Scriptures (Lev. 10:2; Mal. 3:2-3, etc.), seems to make allusion, not to the power of the Spirit, but to His purifying action, which judges and consumes all impurity. The Holy Spirit convicts of sin and of judgment, and He burns within us all that which is not in conformity with the will of God.

Note that the two passages related above, where Matthew and Luke refer to the words of John the Baptist, "He will baptize you with the Holy Ghost and with fire," are immediately followed by a very clear allusion to the fire of eternal judgment. On the other hand, Mark 1:8 and John 1:33 speak in the same terms of the baptism of the Spirit, not having mentioned the fire; neither do they make any allusion to the judgment. Combine with this the very words of Jesus with regard to Hell-fire: "For everyone shall be salted with fire" (Mark 9:49), and those of Paul, "The fire shall try every man's work of what sort it is. If any man's work shall be burned, he shall suffer loss, but he himself shall be saved yet so as by fire" (I Cor. 3:13-15). The repentant sinner shall see sin judged and consumed within him by the Spirit who will regenerate and sanctify him; his work will be judged on the last day, and all imperfections consumed by fire. On the contrary, he who refuses to be saved and purified will be cast into eternal fire. Thus, if we pray to be "baptized with fire" it means asking God to consume the sin within us.

V. LIVING WATERS

Jesus Himself used this image when He said, "He that believeth on me as the Scripture hath said, out of his body shall flow rivers of living water." He spoke of the Spirit "which they that believed on him were to receive" (John 7:38-39). The Saviour also declared to the Samaritan woman, referring without doubt to the Spirit who will come to live in the heart of the believer: "The water that I shall give him shall become in him a well of water springing up into everlasting life" (John 4:14). And again, in Isaiah 44:3 we read: "For I will pour out my Spirit upon thy seed."

This symbol is easy to understand. As living water, the presence of the Spirit in our heart refreshes and quenches thirst; it causes life to appear where reigned beforehand only desolation and death; it brings fullness and plenty and an outpouring of abundant blessing.

In this connection, we see an allusion to the Trinity in Exodus 17:6: "The Lord said to Moses . . . Behold, I will stand before thee, there upon the rock in Horeb; and thou shalt smite the rock, and there shall come water out of it, that the people may drink." Paul clearly tells us that the rock smitten for the salvation of the people was Christ (I Cor. 10:4). As to the living water, we have just seen that it frequently represents the Holy Spirit. This provides a striking image of the manner in which the three divine Persons collaborate in the work of our salvation.

VI. THE SEAL

When we believe, we are sealed by the Holy Spirit for the day of redemption (Eph. 1:13; 4:30; II Cor. 1:22). Among the Jews, the seal was a token of the completion of a transaction; and when the agreement was concluded, the act passed and the price paid, the seal was appended to the contract to make it definite (Jer. 32:9-10). Thus the Holy Spirit becomes the divine stamp upon us, the mark of God's property. He imparts to us the assurance that we are saved and chosen for the day of glory, when our redemption will be perfected.

VII. THE EARNEST

"Ye believe and ye were sealed with the Holy Spirit of promise which is the earnest of our inheritance" (Eph. 1:13-14).

"Now he which stablished us with you in Christ, and hath anointed us, is God; who has also sealed us, and given the earnest of the Spirit in our hearts" (II Cor. 1:21-22).

This image helps us to understand that the actual gift of the Holy Spirit is a solemn guarantee, and is like the first installment of our full salvation. If we have received the Spirit, we can now rely upon this wonderful certainty, and be filled with joy at the thought of the moment when we shall be effectively "filled unto all the fullness of God."

In terminating this chapter on the symbols of the Holy Spirit, may we thank God for helping us by these images to a better understanding of many precious truths and may we endeavor to realize them through faith.

Part II

THE WORK OF THE HOLY SPIRIT
BEFORE PENTECOST

CHAPTER 1

THE HOLY SPIRIT IN THE OLD TESTAMENT

I. HIS PART IN THE CREATION

THE HOLY SPIRIT is God and He is the Spirit of life; it is natural that He should take part in the creation, and in the second verse of Genesis, He is mentioned. "The Spirit of God moved upon the face of the waters."

In the account of the creation, another allusion to the Trinity, and indirectly to the Spirit, is found in the two following expressions: (1) In Genesis 1:1 the Hebrew word "God" is in the plural although the verb is in the singular. It is the same as if the text were to say: "In the beginning, the Gods created." (2) In verse 26: "Let us make [plural] man in our image." The Son is also included in this plural, and besides this we know the part He played in the creation (John 1:3, 10; Heb. 1:10; etc.).

There are several passages which underline the creating power of the Spirit: Genesis 2:7: "The Lord God formed man . . . He breathed into his nostrils the breath [spirit] of life, and man became a living soul." Genesis 6:3: "My Spirit shall not strive with man forever, yet shall his days be an hundred and twenty years." Therefore, life is communicated and maintained by the Spirit. Other texts confirm this, such as Psalm 104:29-30: "Thou takest away their breath, they die. . . . Thou sendest forth thy Spirit, they are created." Job 33:4: "The Spirit of God hath made me, and the breath of the Almighty giveth me life." Ezekiel 37:10: "The breath came unto them, and they lived." John 6:63: "It is the Spirit that

29

quickeneth" (that giveth life). II Corinthians 3:6: "The letter [the law] killeth, but the Spirit giveth life." We shall soon see that the Spirit imparts spiritual life. It is therefore not surprising that He can also give physical life.

II. HIS WORK IN THE HEART OF MEN OF THE OLD COVENANT

Before Jesus was glorified and before Pentecost, the Spirit was not poured out upon all flesh. "The Holy Ghost was not yet given; because Jesus was not yet glorified" (John 7:39); in the Old Covenant, His work in the heart of men was therefore altogether different from what it is now. It was characterized in this way:

1. The Spirit was not given to all.

God clothed with His Spirit those whom He called to a special ministry, such as:

Bezaleel, for the construction of the tabernacle (Exod. 31:3).

Othniel, Gideon, Jephthah, etc., to be judges (Judges 3:10; 6:34; 11:29).

David to be king (I Sam. 16:13).

The prophets, to write the Bible (I Peter 1:10-11).

But it is never said that every Israelite received personally the Holy Spirit. On the contrary, the Old Testament announces that this grace will only be granted under the New Covenant (see 3).

2. The Spirit was temporarily given, and could be withdrawn.

The Old Testament mentions several examples: Samson was under the control of the Spirit from the time of Judges 13:25, until God withdrew from Him (Judges 16:20). Saul also had been laid hold of by the Spirit, who afterwards withdrew Himself from him (I Sam. 10:10; 16:14). Ezekiel relates that the Lord spoke to him. "And the Spirit entered into me when he spake unto me, and set me upon my feet" (2:2). The same scene is reproduced in the following chapter, and the Spirit enters into him again (3:24). Therefore, He did not stay the first time, and we do not know whether He stayed the second time.

That is why David, after his fall, begs God not to withdraw His Holy Spirit from Him (Psa. 51:11). Such a prayer is not found in the New Testament, as the Holy Spirit now lives eternally within us (John 14:16-17). The temporary and even unexpected nature of the reception of the Holy Spirit in the Old Testament is again underlined by the frequently repeated expression: "The Spirit of the Lord came upon David [or some other person]." This is said, for example, of Samson on three occasions: in the incident of the lion, at Ashkelon and at Lehi (Judges 14:6, 19; 15:14), as if, during the interval, the Spirit did not possess him in the same manner. Here are further examples of the sudden descent of the Spirit: "The Spirit of God came upon the messengers of Saul and also prophesied" (I Sam. 19:20). "Then the Spirit came upon Amasai . . . and he said . . ." (I Chron. 12:18). "Then upon Jahaziel . . . came the Spirit of the Lord in the midst of the congregation; and he said . . ." (II Chron. 20:14).

3. Before the cross and Pentecost the Spirit could not do in men what He is doing now.

Christ having not yet died and been raised for sinners, the Spirit could not raise them up with Him. He could not make them members of the Body of Christ, which did not then exist; consequently, He could neither baptize them into one Body (I Cor. 12:13), nor live eternally within them. The Spirit had to find hearts purified from sin before making them His temple. Christ, being without sin, was the first in whom the Spirit made His abode, and if He now lives within us, it is because of the blood of the Lamb which cleanses us from all our sins. But the atonement was not yet accomplished for believers under the Old Covenant. This is the reason why we must understand the real meaning of the following expressions, when they are applied to men of the Old Testament.

In discussing later regeneration, baptism, indwelling and

sanctification, we shall have further evidences of the totally new work done by the Spirit since Pentecost.

"Joshua . . . a man in whom is the Spirit" (Num. 27:18). "The Spirit of Christ which was in them" (the prophets) (I Peter 1:11). "I have filled him [Bezaleel] with the Spirit of God" (Exod. 31:3). "I truly am full of power by the Spirit of the Lord" (Micah 3:8).

In reality, the Spirit could be within these men and even fill them momentarily (as Elisabeth and Zacharias, Luke 1: 41, 67), and nevertheless only act in accordance with the Old Covenant.

Without a doubt, this is the reason why the above expressions are exceptional in the Old Testament. Very frequently, the text declares that the Spirit was not within but upon someone: "The Lord . . . took of the Spirit that was upon him [Moses] and put it upon the seventy elders" (Num. 11:25). "The Spirit of the Lord came upon Othniel, upon Jephthah" (Judges 3:10; 11:29).

We have just stated that in the Old Covenant, the Spirit accomplished an incomplete work in the heart of those upon whom He rested. Then what is the meaning of the text (I Sam. 10:9), "When he [Saul] had turned his back . . . God gave him another heart"? God without a doubt transformed his heart, but this does not necessarily mean that He regenerated it. The tragic end of Saul, rejected by the Lord, in any case shows that he had not received eternal life, which never ceases.

4. The Spirit acted upon the whole nation of Israel, but had not constituted it into one body as He did for the Church later on.

Haggai 2:5 reveals that the Spirit was already to a certain degree with Israel: "I am with you . . . according to the word that I covenanted with you . . . and my Spirit abideth [marg.] among you."

Nehemiah declares: "Thou gavest also a good Spirit to instruct them, . . . and testifiedst against them by thy Spirit through thy prophets" (9:20, 30).

Isaiah expresses himself in these terms: "But they rebelled, and grieved his Holy Spirit: therefore he was turned to be their enemy, and himself fought against them. Then he remembered the days of old, Moses and his people . . . Where is he that put his Holy Spirit in the midst of them? . . . As the cattle that go down into the valley, the Spirit of the Lord caused them to rest" (63:10-11, 14).

These indications have nothing that should surprise us. We have already seen (page 29) that even physical life cannot be created or maintained without the Holy Spirit. Consequently, it is not astonishing that already under the Old Covenant the Spirit exerted a certain influence on the chosen people. Does not God say that all is produced not by might nor by power, but by His Spirit? (Zech. 4:6).

It is nevertheless evident that the action of the Spirit upon the whole nation of Israel was as yet incomplete, the same as His work in the heart of individuals. Christ had to die, "that he should gather together in one the children of God that were scattered abroad" (John 11:52), before the Holy Spirit could be truly given and able to constitute the Church which would collectively become the Body of Christ and the habitation of God through the Spirit. Also the children of Israel were not all pleasing to God, whereas the Church, the temple of the Spirit, can only be composed of individuals truly regenerated.

5. Lastly, the sovereignty of the Spirit is very clearly shown to us in the Old Testament.

"The wind blows where it listeth." The Spirit acts as it pleases Him, and He uses, not only servants of God, but also, at times His enemies. "Balaam lifted up his eyes . . . and the Spirit of God came upon him" (Num. 24:2).

"The Spirit of God came upon the messengers of Saul [sent to kill David], and they also prophesied . . . the Spirit of God came upon him [Saul] also," (already rejected of God and coming himself to kill David) (I Sam. 19:20-23).

It is the same today. The Spirit of God can glorify Himself through whom He will and, if necessary, compel men to serve His purpose.

III. THE ROLE OF THE HOLY SPIRIT IN THE NEW COVENANT, AS IT IS PROCLAIMED IN THE OLD TESTAMENT

Though it is true that before Pentecost the action of the Holy Spirit in the heart of man was incomplete, His future role is clearly announced by the prophets.

1. The Holy Spirit will be poured out upon all flesh (Joel 2:28-29) and upon the house of Israel (Isaiah 44:3; Ezek. 39:29, etc.).

The gift of the Holy Spirit will therefore be linked with promises which are both explicit and universal, as also with precise conditions of faith and obedience; it will no longer be reserved only for isolated individuals of a privileged race. "For to you is the promise, and to your children, and to all that are afar off" (Acts 2:39).

2. The Spirit thus given will remain forever.

"This is my covenant [future] with them, said the Lord; My Spirit . . . and my words . . . shall not depart out of thy mouth, . . . nor out of the mouth of thy seed's seed [thy children's children], saith the Lord, from henceforth and forever" (Isa. 59:21).

3. The Spirit shall live in the heart of man to renew and sanctify it.

"I will put my Spirit in you and ye shall live" (Ezek. 37:14). "A new heart also will I give you, and a new Spirit will I put within you . . . I will put my Spirit within you, and cause you to walk in my statutes" (Ezek. 36:26, 27).

Until then, God had condescended to place His presence in a temple of stone; but under the new covenant, He places it in the hearts of believers who become His temple (I Cor. 3: 16). (The Old Testament does not make known the work of the Spirit in the Body of Christ, since the mystery of the Church was only revealed to the apostles of Christ [Eph. 3: 4-5].)

Besides this, God had written His law on tables of stone; soon He would put His law in the spirit and heart of men, by the Holy Spirit:

"This is the covenant that I will make . . . I will put my law in their inward parts, and in their heart will I write it" (Jer. 31:33).

Paul also wrote, "Ye are . . . being made manifest that ye are an epistle of Christ, . . . written . . . with the Spirit of the living God; not in tables of stone, but in tables that are hearts of flesh" (II Cor. 3:3). Then, thanks to His power, man can put into practice the will of God and be sanctified, being freed from the letter [of the law] which killeth, but transformed by the Spirit who giveth life (see II Cor. 3:6).

All these promises could not be fulfilled until after the completion of the redemptive work of Christ. Not until Christ was crucified, raised again and glorified, could the Spirit be poured out and accomplish all His work (John 7:39; 16:7, etc.).

4. The Spirit shall rest upon the Messiah, Mediator of the New Covenant.

Paul called the New Covenant the Covenant of the Spirit (II Cor. 3:6). Therefore, its Mediator must possess the Spirit without measure.

"The Spirit of the Lord shall rest upon him, the Spirit of wisdom and understanding, the Spirit of counsel and might, the Spirit of knowledge and of the fear of the Lord . . . Behold my servant . . . I have put my Spirit upon him; he shall bring forth judgment to the Gentiles . . . The Spirit of the Lord is upon me; because the Lord hath anointed me to preach good tidings unto the meek" (Isa. 11:2; 42:1; 61:1).

CONCLUSION

The Old Testament already speaks very clearly of the Spirit and of His work in the past, the present and the future, that is to say at the creation, in the Old and New Covenants. The Spirit gives life, performs miracles, works in the heart of men, using them as His instruments; in short, nothing is accomplished without Him, and all is brought to pass with His help. God's Word sums it all up in this way: "Not by might, nor by power but by my Spirit, saith the Lord of hosts" (Zech. 4:6).

CHAPTER 2

THE HOLY SPIRIT IN THE GOSPELS

THE GOSPELS represent a period of transition in the Scriptures. Christ the Mediator of the New Covenant has come down to earth. By His words and His deeds He lays the basis of the future dispensation which is only to begin after the crucifixion, the resurrection and the glorification of the Saviour. The Church was not founded until Pentecost, by the descent of the Holy Spirit. In the Gospels, the result is that generally the teaching and promises of Jesus concerning the Spirit refer to the New Covenant, whereas the experiences realized by the forerunners and the disciples still belong to the Old. If we take careful note of this difference, we shall be guarded against confusion.

I. THE WORK OF THE SPIRIT IN THE HEART OF MAN AS RECORDED IN THE GOSPELS

It is the same as in the Old Testament. Luke gives us the most details on this subject. He records the word of the angel concerning John the Baptist: "He shall be filled with the Holy Ghost, even from his mother's womb"; we also learn that Elisabeth and Zacharias were themselves filled with the Holy Spirit and enabled to prophesy about the Messiah (Luke 1:15, 41, 67). Finally, Luke tells us that "Simeon . . . was righteous and devout . . . and the Holy Spirit was upon him. And it had been revealed unto him by the Holy Spirit that he should not see death before he had seen the Lord's Christ. And he came by the Spirit, into the temple" (2:25-27). These expressions that we have already met with in our chapter upon

37

the work of the Spirit in the Old Testament, refer to experiences such as those belonging to the Old Covenant could have had. But we are still far from the perfect work which the Spirit is accomplishing since Pentecost. Jesus Himself declares that "he that is least in the kingdom of heaven is greater than John the Baptist" (Matt. 11:11).

In the Gospels, the Lord speaks in the future tense of the gift of the Spirit soon to be granted to every believer. See Luke 11:13. So far the Spirit had only been bestowed upon especially chosen instruments; since Christ's coming, all asking for God's grace and presence shall receive them. God reveals Himself in Christ as a Father whose love is infinitely superior to the love of human fathers: to anyone coming to Him as a child, He will give all the good things (Matt. 7:11) and the unspeakable gift of His Spirit.

II. WHAT EXPERIENCE DID THE DISCIPLES HAVE ON THE DAY OF THE RESURRECTION?

According to John 20:19-23, on the day of the resurrection Jesus came and stood in the midst of His disciples and breathing upon them said: "Receive ye the Holy Ghost." If then, as we said in our last paragraph, the Spirit was not fully poured out until Pentecost, what did the disciples receive at that moment? Did the New Covenant already commence for them on Easter Day? In other words, did they receive the complete gift of the Spirit on this day with the exception of His baptism which they experienced at Pentecost? I do not think so.

It seems to me that they received a certain measure of the Spirit on the evening of the resurrection, but that this experience did not then overstep the bounds of the Old Covenant, despite the promises and the orders that accompanied it. (We have sufficiently proved how, in this setting, the Spirit acted in an incomplete way, it is true, but nevertheless a sovereign and varied manner.) In breathing upon His disciples, Jesus gave them in some measure a token of the real gift which they could not fully receive before Pentecost, when they entered into the New Dispensation. It was only a partial, prophetic fulfillment of the great promise of the Spirit. Here are a few proofs.

1. First of all, let us note that before the resurrection the disciples did not yet possess the life of the Spirit.

In His discourse in the Upper Room, Jesus incessantly spoke to them about it in the future tense: "And I will pray the Father, and he shall give you another Comforter, . . . the Spirit of truth . . . [He] shall be in you . . . and he when he is come, will convict, . . . He shall guide you" (John 14:16-17; 16:8, 13; etc.).

2. The Spirit could not be poured out before Jesus was glorified.

Indeed, even at the resurrection "the Spirit was not yet given, because Jesus was not yet glorified" (John 7:39). It was only after being exalted to the right hand of God that He received the Holy Ghost which had been promised by the Father, and which He poured forth (Acts 2:33). On the other hand, in order that believers might have a complete Christian experience, it was necessary that they should be not only raised with Christ but should sit with Him in the heavenly places and be glorified with Him (Eph. 2:6; Rom. 8:30). This was impossible before the ascension of the Saviour.

3. On the resurrection day, Jesus had not yet left His disciples.

Now He had declared, "It is expedient for you that I go away, for if I go not away, the Comforter will not come unto you; but if I go, I will send him unto you" (John 16:7). Since He had not left His disciples on Easter Day, He could not then fulfill His promise.

4. Forty days later, at the ascension, Jesus again exhorted His disciples to await the promise of the Father of which He had spoken (Acts 1:4).

We have seen that which the Father had promised concerning the Spirit in the New Covenant: that He would be given to all forever and that He would be in man to regenerate and sanctify him. Jesus Christ Himself had also announced exactly the same thing (John 14:16-17). Now it is clear that these promises were fulfilled only at Pentecost. On ascension day, Jesus adds further, "Ye shall receive power when the Holy Ghost is come upon you" (Acts 1:8). Therefore the disciples had not yet received Him in the manner He wished for them.

5. According to Acts 1:5 the disciples were not baptized with the Spirit until Pentecost.

As we shall see later, the baptism of the Spirit is the act by which God places the believer in Jesus Christ and makes him a member of His Body (I Cor. 12:13). Consequently, before this experience, the disciples were not yet "in Christ" and had not received the new nature (because one must be "in Christ" to become a new creature [II Cor. 5:17]). Therefore, they had not passed over the true threshold of the New Covenant before Pentecost.

6. Since the Body of Christ was not yet constituted, the disciples could not receive the life which comes from Christ, the Head (Eph. 4:16).

They were not "in Christ" but Christ was not yet "within them" either.

7. We must not forget that the disciples belonged to two dispensations.

Even though they had received a certain measure of the Spirit before receiving the baptism at Pentecost, their experience cannot be in any way the standard one for us. Also, whatever may be the explanation that we give of John 20:22, it would be impossible for us to say: "The disciples firstly 'received the Spirit,' then fifty days later they were 'baptized with the Holy Ghost,' therefore we also, after having received the Spirit at the time of our regeneration, should seek and receive His baptism later on." Indeed, not one of us has belonged to the Old Covenant and we should cling solely to the teaching that concerns the New Dispensation. (We shall return to this subject in our chapter on the baptism of the Holy Spirit.)

CHAPTER 3

THE WORK OF THE HOLY SPIRIT IN JESUS CHRIST

JESUS CHRIST was assisted by the Spirit throughout His whole life upon earth.

I. CHRIST WAS BORN OF THE HOLY SPIRIT

The angel Gabriel announced to Mary that the Son to be born to her would be conceived of the Holy Spirit (Luke 1: 35); and God made known to Joseph that the child whom Mary had conceived was of the Holy Ghost (Matt. 1:20). It is for this reason that He is at the same time Man and God. Without this truth, the Gospel would break down, because His humanity and His divinity are both indispensable, one as much as the other to our salvation.

II. HE WAS ANOINTED WITH THE HOLY SPIRIT

Christ Himself declared: "The Son can do nothing of himself, but what he seeth the Father doing" (John 5:19). Therefore, He was anointed with the Holy Spirit, in view of the ministry that He was to undertake.

Jesus affirms this in quoting a prophecy from Isaiah: "The Spirit of the Lord is upon me, because he anointed me to preach good tidings to the poor" (Luke 4:18). This is confirmed by Acts 10:38: "God anointed him [Jesus of Nazareth] with the Holy Ghost and with power: who went about doing good ... for God was with him."

As we have seen previously, the Old Testament clearly announced that the Messiah would be clothed with the Holy Spirit. The priests and the kings received an unction of oil

41

(Lev. 8:12 and I Sam. 16:12-13) and this fact foreshadowed that Jesus Christ, the King of kings and the High Priest of the New Covenant, would be anointed with the Holy Spirit. Still clearer prophecies are found in Isaiah: "And there shall come forth a shoot out of the stock of Jesse ... the Spirit of the Lord shall rest upon him: the Spirit of wisdom and understanding, the Spirit of counsel and might, the Spirit of knowledge and of the fear of the Lord" (Isa. 11:1-2); "Behold my servant ... my chosen, in whom my soul delighteth. I have put my Spirit upon him" (Isa. 42:1). (Look again at Isaiah 61:1 recently quoted.) Finally, this is what is expressed in Psalm 45: 7, quoted in Hebrews 1:9: "Therefore God, thy God, hath anointed thee with the oil of gladness above thy fellows." And Psalm 2:6: "Yet I have set [French version *anointed*] my king upon my holy hill of Zion."

III. HE WAS SEALED BY THE HOLY SPIRIT

Speaking of the Son of Man, Jesus declares: "For him the Father ... hath sealed" (John 6:27). This seal upon Him was the mark of His heavenly origin and the proof of His divine Sonship.

IV. THE SPIRIT LIVED IN HIM

In speaking of His body, Jesus said, "Destroy this temple, and in three days I will raise it up" (John 2:19). He certainly meant that He was the temple of the Holy Spirit, as the believer also by faith becomes His temple. Besides, it is written that at His baptism the Spirit descended and remained upon Him (John 1:33). We do not here attempt to solve the question of knowing in what measure the Spirit was in Christ before His baptism in Jordan. Since it was not necessary for Him to be regenerated, He certainly had the Holy Spirit already. At the beginning of His ministry, the Spirit came upon Him in a more definite manner, to permit Him to accomplish His task. At any rate, the Spirit lived in Him and with Him. This is what Jesus Christ Himself meant when on several occasions He declared that the Father was in Him (John 10:38; 14:11). God's Spirit was in Him, even as He lives in our hearts (Eph. 2:22: "Ye . . . are . . . a habitation of God in the Spirit.").

V. CHRIST WAS FILLED WITH THE HOLY SPIRIT

According to John 3:34, God did not give the Spirit by measure; and we read in Luke 4:1 that Jesus returned from Jordan filled with the Holy Spirit. Since no sin separated Him from His Father and all Christ's will was submitted to Him, it is evident that the Spirit filled His whole being.

VI. HE WAS CLOTHED WITH THE POWER OF THE SPIRIT

Jesus Himself said that the result of the fullness of the Spirit is that rivers of living waters flow out (John 7:38) and that power is manifested outside. It was in this manner that the Saviour, clothed with the power of the Spirit according to Luke 4:14, was able to fulfill His ministry. He had been anointed with the Holy Spirit and with power (Acts 10:38) and it was with this power that He accomplished all He did upon earth. For example, He explicitly declares that it is by the Spirit of God that He casts out devils (Matt. 12:28); and He adds that the Father who dwells in Him does the works (John 14:10). It is also through the Holy Ghost that He gives His commands to the disciples (Acts 1:2).

These affirmations assume all their significance if we remember that Jesus Christ is the One to whom belongs all power, and by whom the whole universe was created (John 1:3, 10).

VII. HE WAS LED BY THE SPIRIT

"Jesus was led by the Spirit in the wilderness, during forty days, being tempted of the devil" (Luke 4:1-2). This guidance of the Spirit was evidently constant in His life and the obedience of the Son toward Him permitted Him to say: "He that sent me is with me; he hath not left me alone: for I do always those things that are pleasing to him" (John 8:29). Without going further than the text, we can also say that Jesus was unceasingly taught by the Spirit and guided by Him into all truth. "I do nothing of myself; but as the Father taught me, I speak these things" (John 8:28). It was with this end in view that God made the Spirit of wisdom, understanding, counsel and might, knowledge and the fear of the Lord to rest upon Him (Isa. 11:2).

VIII. THE FRUIT OF THE SPIRIT ABOUNDED IN CHRIST

"The fruit of the Spirit is love, joy, peace, long-suffering, kindness, goodness, faithfulness, meekness and temperance" (Gal. 5:22). All these virtues were only perfectly possessed by Jesus Christ. But the power of the Spirit was party to this fact, since it is said, for example: "He [Jesus] rejoiced in the Holy Spirit, and said, I thank thee, O Father" (Luke 10:21). It was for this reason that not only His joy, but also His peace, love, and patience remained perfect even in the midst of the most terrible suffering.

IX. IT WAS BY THE SPIRIT THAT HE OFFERED HIMSELF AS A SACRIFICE

The assistance of the Spirit was necessary to Him in His voluntary humiliation: "Christ, who through the eternal Spirit offered himself without blemish unto God" (Heb. 9:14).

X. FINALLY CHRIST WAS RAISED BY THE SPIRIT

It was also the Spirit of God who raised Christ from the grave: "If the Spirit of Him that raised up Jesus from the dead dwelleth in you, He that raised up Christ Jesus from the dead shall also quicken your mortal bodies through His Spirit that dwelleth within you" (Rom. 8:11). The meaning of this verse is evident: The Spirit of God lived in Christ and raised Him; if the same Spirit lives in you, He will also raise you. Lastly see Romans 1:4 and I Timothy 3:16; Christ by His resurrection was declared to be the Son of God with power according to the Spirit of holiness who thus justified Him in the eyes of all.

CONCLUSION

Even from before His birth and until after His death, in other words, during all His ministry upon earth, Christ chose to have need of the assistance and the power of the Spirit. We can draw from this fact two essential conclusions:

1. Although Jesus Christ was God come down to earth, He was also perfectly man and could "do nothing of himself."

2. The living Son of God, in all His unequaled greatness, chose not to do without the help of the Spirit even for one day.

How can we, poor sinful and powerless creatures, hope to live a Christian life without the presence and the fullness of the same Spirit? May God preserve us from such foolish presumption! Indeed, Christ was born of the Spirit; He was anointed and sealed with the Spirit who lived within Him and filled Him; the fruit of the Spirit abounded in Him; He was clothed with His power and led by Him. Finally, it was by the Spirit that He offered Himself as a sacrifice and that He was raised up. All these experiences we can and must make ourselves in the degree that God has indicated for us, otherwise we cannot be true Christians. "He that saith he abideth in him ought himself also to walk, even as he walked" (I John 2:6).

We must be born again by the Spirit and receive His unction and His seal. He wants to live in us, fill us and clothe us with His power, produce His fruit in us, and lead us step by step. It is also by Him that we should offer up a living sacrifice which will be on our part a reasonable service, and finally, it is by Him that we shall be raised from the dead. Have we thought upon these things, and have they become living realities to us? It is a matter of our eternal salvation.

(It is interesting to note that the Scripture never says that Jesus was baptized with the Spirit with whom He was clothed and filled. Since the baptism of the Spirit, as we shall see later on, aims at making us members of the Body of Christ, I Corinthians 12:13, it is evident that the Saviour did not need it, and could not be joined to His own Body.)

CHAPTER 4

THE HOLY SPIRIT AND THE INSPIRATION OF THE BIBLE

THE SCRIPTURE distinctly affirms that the sacred books were not composed by men according to their fancy or their own ideas. Their authors were inspired and guided by the Spirit who alone searches and reveals the deep things of God (I Cor. 2:9-11), so that their writings afford us all the desired guarantees.

"For no prophecy ever came by the will of man: but men spake from God being moved by the Holy Ghost" (II Peter 1:21). "Concerning which salvation the prophets . . . searched diligently . . . searching what time . . . the Spirit of Christ which was in them did point unto, when it testified beforehand the sufferings of Christ, and the glories that should follow them" (I Peter 1:10-11).

We also find in the Old Testament affirmations such as this:

"The Spirit of the Lord spake by me, and His word was upon my tongue" (II Sam. 23:2).

And all the prophets from Moses to Malachi, declare, "Thus spake the Lord," or "saith the Lord," or again, "The word of the Lord came unto me, saying." Now without the Spirit these men would not have had a single revelation.

Christ also speaks of David as being "in the Spirit" (Matt. 22:43), and the New Testament speaks of the Old in the following manner:

"It was needful that the Scripture should be fulfilled, which the Holy Ghost spake . . . by the mouth of David" (Acts 1:16). "O Lord . . . who by the Holy Ghost, by the mouth of our father David thy servant didst say" (Acts 4:24, 25). "Well spake the Holy Ghost by Isaiah the prophet unto your fathers" (Acts 28:25). "The Holy Ghost this signifying [in Exodus and Leviticus], that the way into the holy place hath not yet been made manifest" (Heb. 9:8).

Jesus explicitly stated that the New Testament, as well as the Old, was inspired by the Spirit.

"The Comforter . . . shall teach you all things, and bring to your remembrance, all that I said unto you" (John 14:26). "He shall guide you into all the truth . . . and he shall declare unto you the things that are to come" (John 16:13, which Jesus could not yet reveal to the disciples who were insufficiently prepared, and that we find in the rest of the New Testament).

Besides, Paul declares that he as well as the apostles and prophets of the New Covenant have received the revelation of all the counsel of God: "Unto us, God revealed them [these things] through the Spirit" (I Cor. 2:10). The mystery of Christ "hath now been revealed unto his holy apostles and prophets in the Spirit" (Eph. 3:5). "The Spirit saith expressly, that in later times some shall fall away from the faith" (I Tim. 4:1).

The Gospel "now is manifested and by the Scriptures of the prophets, according to the commandment of the eternal God" (Rom. 16:26). All these writings are therefore inspired by God.

Because they are inspired, let us approach the writings of Scripture with all respect and take care not to sin by unbelief against the Holy Spirit who is the Author.

But, it may be asked, has the Spirit inspired all the passages of the Bible? Yes, because "every Scripture is inspired of God and is also profitable for teaching" (II Tim. 3:16). This is why it is strictly forbidden to take away from or to add anything to it, under penalty of losing one's part in the tree of life (Rev. 22:18-19). (This does not exclude the fact that the Bible revelation is progressive and that the Spirit speaks in a much more explicit and complete manner, for example, in the New Testament than at the beginning of the Old.)

Did the Spirit inspire only in a general sense, or did He guide the authors in the choice of the words to be employed? It is difficult for us to be more precise than the Scripture itself. But in I Corinthians 2:12-13 Paul declares: "We speak not in words which man's wisdom teacheth, but which the Spirit teacheth; comparing spiritual things with spiritual." Since every idea is expressed in words, it would be difficult to imagine an inspiration that did not in some way bear upon the form in which the truth should be expressed. This naturally applies to the original text. Did this mean that divine inspiration swept aside the personality of the authors of the sacred writings? Certainly not, as we can recognize immediately through their writings the style and even the temperament of David, Paul, John, and the others. On the contrary, the Spirit developed their personality while respecting it, and led them into all truth.

The Spirit who guided the authors of the sacred book is also He who directs the sincere reader of the Scriptures. He teaches him all things and also leads him into all truth, meaning that He explains the word which is the truth (John 14:26; 16:13; 17:17). We shall return to this particular point when we study the teaching work of the Spirit. But we ought here to emphasize the importance of reading and studying the Bible. Since the Spirit Himself is the Author, how much we sadden Him by neglecting the treasures of wisdom and strength that He through His Holy Word wishes to impart to us! If His power is to be made manifest anew among us, it is of primary importance that His message should regain its due place. Then we shall be able to put the enemy to flight by the sword of the Spirit which is the Word of God (Eph. 6:17).

Part III

THE WORK OF THE HOLY SPIRIT IN THE HEART OF MAN SINCE PENTECOST

CHAPTER 1

THE DISPENSATION OF THE SPIRIT

THE APOSTLE PAUL making a comparison between the Old Covenant, based on the law, and the New based on the Gospel of grace, speaks of it thus: "God . . . also made us sufficient as ministers of the new covenant, not of the letter [that is, the law], but of the Spirit: for the letter killeth but the Spirit giveth life. But if the ministration of death, written and engraven on stones [the tables of the law], came with glory . . . how shall not rather the ministration of the Spirit be with glory?" (II Cor. 3:6-8). We are therefore in this present time and since Pentecost in the dispensation of the Spirit.

I. THE SPIRIT FREES THE BELIEVER FROM THE LAW OF SIN AND EMPOWERS HIM TO LIVE

The law revealed to men only the will of God without any supply of power wherewith to put it into practice. On the contrary, it condemned him to death by the knowledge that failure to observe every detail of the law brought him under a curse (Gal. 3:10). For this very reason Paul calls the law "the letter which killeth" and again the "ministration of death." On the other hand, the Spirit regenerates the sinner, dead in his transgressions, and frees him from the law of sin by imparting to him power to live (Rom. 8:2).

II. THE SPIRIT PUTS GOD'S LAW IN THE BELIEVER'S HEART

From many points of view the Old Covenant was material and fleshly; to this we find a reference in Hebrews 7:16. God's presence, the "Shekinah," dwelt in a temple of stone, and His law was on graven tables. But now, through the Spirit, He dwells in the hearts of all believers and puts His law in them. "Ye are of Christ, ministered by us, written not with ink but with the Spirit of the living God; not in tables of stone, but in tables that are hearts of flesh" (I Cor. 3:16; II Cor. 3:3).

III. THE SPIRIT EFFECTS A CIRCUMCISION OF HEART

In the Old Covenant, the fact of belonging to God was marked by circumcision of the flesh; in the New by the circumcision of the heart, that is to say, the regeneration brought about by the Spirit. "Neither is that circumcision [which counts before God] which is outward in the flesh; [but] . . . that of the heart, in the Spirit, not in the letter [the law]" (Rom. 2: 28, 29). "For we are the circumcision, who worship by the Spirit of God and glory in Christ Jesus" (Phil. 3:3).

IV. THE SPIRIT'S MINISTRY IS BASED ON CHRIST'S WORK

It is evident that the whole ministry of the Spirit is based upon the work of Jesus Christ. The Spirit seeks to glorify Him (John 16:13-14). That we might "walk in the Spirit" God sent, because of sin, His own Son in the flesh like unto that of the sinful (Rom. 8:3, 4). Through His death on the cross, Christ has taken away our sin and has crucified with Himself the old man within us. By His resurrection He has made us live anew with Him, and in His glorification He reassumed His sovereign place at God's right hand, whence He sends the Spirit to us. And moreover, it is He Himself who with His redemptive work concluded, places within us His spiritual presence. Thus without Christ, salvation is impossible. But with the exclusion of the ministry of the Spirit, this salvation so dearly and perfectly wrought could not be imparted to us personally, since it would not be within us.

From this viewpoint we can distinguish three dispensations in the divine plan.

First, the Father's Dispensation, which is found in the Old Testament. Here it is the Father who reveals Himself, acting without an intermediary. He is "God *for* us" ready to bless and to succor but nevertheless remaining far above in the heavens on account of His formidable greatness, His holiness and the sin of man. Wherefore Isaiah exclaimed: "Oh that thou wouldest rend the heavens, that thou wouldest come down" (Isa. 64:1).

Second, the Son's Dispensation, that of the Gospels. The Father has hearkened unto the cry of lost humanity; He manifests His love by sending upon earth His Son who becomes "God *with* us, Emmanuel." In this period of time Jesus Christ reveals Himself, He speaks, He acts and comes forward to receive man's adoration. He achieves the world's salvation and then returns in glory to His Father's side, waiting until He shall come to reign a thousand years here on earth.

Third, the Dispensation of the Holy Spirit, which, starting at Pentecost, will last until the Saviour's return. During this time, the Spirit molds the Church and becomes "God *in* us." He convicts the world of sin and imparts to the believer's heart all that Christ has won for him: His pardon, His life, His victory, His power, His very presence.

Yet again it must be stressed that the three Persons of the Trinity are indivisible, even when, in the course of a dispensation, the major role is taken by one of the Trinity. We have already studied the Holy Spirit's action in the Father's dispensation and we know that the Son also is constantly present in the Old Testament whether it be in prophecies or by direct intervention. In the Son's Dispensation the Father upholds Him and confirms His work, while the Spirit bears Him constant company. Lastly, in the Dispensation of the Spirit, the three Persons of the Divinity together act in the world, dwelling both in the Church and in the believer's heart. Thus it is impossible that one of the Trinity should supersede the two other Persons, or sever their perfect unity or their close association.

May we in no way hinder the full working of all three Persons of the Trinity in our lives and may we receive the full salvation which only the Three in unity can accord us!

CHAPTER 2

THE CONVICTION BROUGHT
ABOUT BY THE SPIRIT

THE SIN AGAINST THE HOLY SPIRIT

I. THE WORK OF CONVICTION

WE NOW COME to the study of the work of the Spirit in man since Pentecost. What is His primary task in the heart of one not yet converted?

1. The Holy Spirit convicts of sin.

"And he, when he is come, will convict the world in respect of sin . . . because they believe not on me" (John 16:8, 9). Thus it is clear that man must recognize that he is in a state of sin and perdition before he can accept the Saviour who will deliver him from it. It is a sick man, who, acknowledging his illness, seeks a doctor (Mark 2:17).

The Holy Spirit convicts the world, that is to say all men, of sin. There is none to whom He does not impart a sense of guilt, whether it be through the Scriptures or simply by his conscience (Rom. 2:14, 15).

Note that in John 16:8, 9, the word *sin* is in the singular and not in the plural. The Spirit reveals to man his state of perdition but not on the grounds that he has committed certain faults or even certain crimes (though, in truth, God in His Word does promise pardon for all sins to him who believes. "Though your sins be as scarlet, they shall be as white as snow" [Isa. 1:18]). Man is condemned before God not because he is a sinner but because, being in a state of sin, he has refused to believe in the Saviour and accept His pardon. "He that believeth not hath been judged already, because he hath not believed on the name of the only begotten Son of God" (John 3:18). Unbelief, when brought face to face with Jesus Christ, is the most serious sin which man can commit.

This sin is unpardonable for the very reason that it consists of a voluntary and obstinate refusal to accept pardon. God will never force any man to believe against his will, for He created man as a free being.

2. The Spirit then brings conviction concerning righteousness.

"Because," said Jesus, "I go to the Father, and ye behold me no more" (John 16:8, 10). Not only does the Spirit show man his state of perdition, but reveals to him at the same time Jesus Christ, whose righteousness and divinity are proved by His resurrection and return to the Father's side. Thus God convinces a heart that is sincere in its repentance that Jesus is of a truth the Saviour who being Himself just, will justify those who in faith depend on Him (Rom. 5:19). Here again, according to John 16:8, it is the world, or in other words, all men, who will receive this conviction through the Spirit. All those who come into contact with the Gospel must, at one time or another, acknowledge that it is the truth and that Jesus is indeed the Saviour. Herein lies their responsibility before God if despite this they persistently refuse to accept His salvation.

3. Finally, He brings conviction of judgment.

"Because the prince of this world hath been judged" (John 16:8, 11). If a man sets his face against that double conviction which the Holy Spirit would work within him, he will be convicted under judgment. How can we know that unbelievers will be judged? By the fact that their father, the Devil, is considered judged already. Christ, by His cross, has virtually destroyed him (Heb. 2:14). The Holy Spirit concludes by convincing those who withstand Him that the same punishment will overtake them once they have been cast into the everlasting fire prepared for the Devil and his angels (Matt. 25:41). Conviction with regard to judgment will be such that "every mouth may be stopped" leaving no place for recrimination (Rom. 3:19) and that even the unbelievers in Hell will tremblingly bow the knee before Him whom they have rejected.

Peter's sermon on the day of Pentecost illustrates the manner in which the Holy Spirit seeks to bring conviction to men:

Of sin: by drawing the attention of the Jews to their rejection and crucifixion of Jesus (Acts 2:23).

Of righteousness: by proving to them that Jesus is of a truth the Messiah, the Son of God announced by the Holy Word, resurrected and glorified (Acts 2:22, 24, 36).

Of judgment: by speaking to them of the Lord's return, of that great day of judgment which draws near, heralded by amazing signs, and by exhorting them to save themselves from this perverse generation before it be too late (Acts 2:19, 20, 40).

II. THE SIN AGAINST THE HOLY SPIRIT

1. What is the sin against the Holy Spirit?

First let us turn to those passages in which this expression is used.

"All their sins shall be forgiven unto the sons of men, and their blasphemies wherewith soever they shall blaspheme; but whosoever shall blaspheme against the Holy Spirit hath never forgiveness, but is guilty of an eternal sin" (Mark 3:28-30). Jesus spake thus because they had said, "He hath an unclean spirit." See also Matthew 12:31-32 and Luke 12:10.

It can be readily seen that the sin committed by the Jews on that occasion did not consist solely of the reported comment in Mark 3:30. The words spoken gave expression to an inward attitude, for from the abundance of the heart the mouth speaketh. What was this attitude? From the very beginning of His career, Jesus Christ had preached repentance, and faith in the good news, while multiplying the number of miracles accomplished by the power of the Spirit, to convince the people of the truth of His message. But the Jews elected not to believe, thrusting aside the Spirit's testimony and finding arguments whereby they might deny this evidence. They refused to admit their sinfulness and to accept Christ in the light of a

Saviour. Thus it was that Jesus spoke to them of that sin which cannot be forgiven.

In the example which has been quoted the sin against the Holy Spirit had taken the form of a blasphemy. But other passages would indicate that, in his heart, man can commit the same unpardonable sin without of necessity making it manifest by the use of blasphemous words. Look, for example, at the two following texts:

a. John 12:37-40. Despite all the miracles performed in their presence, the Jews believed not on Him. God therefore abandoned them to their unbelief and its consequences.

b. Hebrews 10:26-31. If a man willingly sins after receiving knowledge of the truth, if he tramples underfoot the Son of God and despises His sacrifice of full atonement, he at the same time outrages most seriously the Spirit of grace who desired to save him. There remains for him nothing further than the fearful expectation of judgment.

We can, therefore, conclude that the sin against the Holy Spirit consists not only of blasphemy against Him but also of a voluntary and decisive refusal to allow that work of salvation which He desires to work within us. (*Decisive* is here used in the sense of final until the opportunity is past, whether by the intervention of death or whether it be that God, wearying of His patience, withdraws Himself from man.) Let us in this connection bear in mind the comment made with regard to John 16:8-9. The greatest sin, of which the Spirit will convict the whole world, is that of unbelief in Jesus. This sin can never be forgiven since it consists of a renouncement of pardon and a rejection of the Saviour. We can thus make this further definition that the sin against the Holy Spirit is to maintain a persistent refusal to believe in Jesus whom the Spirit presents before our souls.

If all depends on our attitude toward Christ, why did Jesus say that all words spoken against the Son of Man would be forgiven, while blasphemy against the Holy Spirit would remain unpardonable? Here is the reason: to sin against God under the law was a serious matter. The sin against Jesus Christ in human form was yet more serious (John 15:22); nevertheless the Son in His humility presented Himself in visible form to men; to repulse Him was still pardonable. But to resist the Spirit who glorifies Him and who gives rise within our hearts to an unmistakably clear conviction is an act of willful sin, willingly and deliberately shutting the door in the face of God. The work of the Spirit, seeking to place within us the Saviour's presence, is the final issue in God's plan for us. If man rejects it and maintains his stubbornness, God can do no more for him; He cannot save him in opposition to his will.

III. WHAT ARE THE CONSEQUENCES OF THE SIN AGAINST THE HOLY SPIRIT?

They are, indeed, terrible.

1. God abandons man to himself.

It is not possible to trifle with God. If man will know nothing of Him, He will forsake him. Here are two striking examples.

a. Immediately after the blasphemy committed by the Jews, Jesus refuses their request for another miracle and starts to speak in parables which He explains only to His disciples (Matt. 12:38-39; 13:10, 13). He declares that it shall not be given to those who will not believe to know the mysteries of the kingdom of Heaven, and that even that which they have shall be taken from them. This is tantamount to saying that God ceases to reveal Himself to those who oppose Him and that by this very act they lose what little spiritual light they may have had.

b. We find another example in Jeremiah. God first describes the people's attitude:

"They have refused to receive correction; they have made their faces harder than a rock; . . . they refuse to return" (5:3; 8:5). They said, "We will not walk therein [in thy ways]

... we will not hearken" (6:16, 17). "I spake unto you, rising up early and speaking, but ye heard not; and I called you but ye answered not" (7:13). "They refuse to know me" (9:6). Then the Lord tells them what He will do: "I will cast you out of my sight" (7:15, 29).

This abandoning is so complete that on four occasions God repeats to the prophet that it is from henceforth of no avail to pray for the people, since He will not hearken.

2. Man's heart is hardened.

It is not God but man himself who of his own volition first hardens his heart. This is clearly seen in the Gospels. That is why Matthew 13:14-15 declares that "their ears are dull of hearing, and their eyes they have closed lest haply they should ... understand with their hearts and should turn again and I should heal them." For whosoever hears the Lord's call and fails to reply, hardens his heart. On this account the Holy Spirit says, "Today if ye shall hear his voice, harden not your hearts" (Heb. 3:7-8).

But if man continues in his resistance against the Spirit, it is God, who in His turn, hardens the heart (John 12:40). The most typical case is perhaps that of Pharaoh. It is recounted that he first hardened his heart six times, refusing to obey God's orders (Exod. 7:13, 22; 8:11, 15, 28; 9:7). And only after that do we then see God hardening the heart of Pharaoh (Exod. 9:12; 10:1, 20, 27; 14:8). Does God have to do great things to harden a heart? It is enough that He should withdraw and cease to strive with man by His Spirit. And what of the future of a heart thus hardened?

3. It becomes impossible for man to repent.

Hebrews 6:6 speaks of men who can no longer be brought to repentance. Matthew 13:15 also states that this obduracy will hinder them from obtaining sight, understanding, and conversion. Evidence makes it plain that if a man rejects all divine aid he will, finally, no longer experience that conviction of sin, which is the work of the Spirit, and the way to Christ will not remain open to him; for no man comes to Jesus save the Father draw him (John 6:44).

Despite contrary appearances, the examples of Esau and Judas confirm what has been written above. Of the ungodly Esau, Hebrews 12:17 comments, "When he afterward desired to inherit the blessing, he was rejected, for he found no place of repentance, though he sought it diligently with tears." But it is easy to see in Genesis 27:38-41 that Esau's tears were motivated by self-interest rather than repentance of sin; his condition was not sincere before God since at the same time his heart was filled with hatred and a desire to kill. As for Judas (Matt. 27:3-5) his penitence contained no godly sorrow leading to a repentance unto salvation which man never regrets, but rather a worldly remorse which brought about his death (II Cor. 7:10). To declare a sin, and to tremble before its consequence, does not indeed constitute true repentance. Nowhere do we read that Judas cried unto God for pardon, and the very fact of his suicide (a crime forbidden by God, Exod. 20:13) gives unfortunate proof that he was not prepared to forsake the path of disobedience. With Peter, however, we have a contrasting proof that a sincere heart, even after sinning gravely, can of a truth repent and obtain pardon.

4. Belief becomes impossible.

"How can ye believe, which receive glory one of another and the glory that cometh from the only God ye seek not?" (John 5:44). "For this cause they could not believe" (John 12:39, 40). Namely, for those very reasons pointed out in connection with repentance. He who chooses to disobey God cannot believe without His help; and yet all that was required of him was to accept the faith which God gives to all those who approach Him in sincerity.

5. Pardon can no longer be secured.

"Whosoever shall blaspheme against the Holy Spirit hath never forgiveness, but is guilty of an eternal sin" (Mark 3:29; Matt. 12:32; Luke 12:10).

"For if we sin willfully after that we have received the knowledge of the truth, there remaineth no more a sacrifice for sins, but a certain fearful expectation of judgment and a fierceness of fire which shall devour the adversaries" (Heb. 10:26, 27). It has already been explained more than once why this impossibility exists: he who, knowing the truth, willfully thrusts aside the work of Christ and of the Holy Spirit cannot be saved by any other power or any other sacrifice. God is not desirous of forcing man to love Him and cannot make a greater offering than that of His Son and His Holy Spirit. Moreover the punishment attendant upon this sin is unending; for it is "an eternal sin." The assurance of everlasting punishment, coupled with Mark 3:28, "All their [other] sins shall be forgiven unto the sons of men," enables us to conclude in short that only those guilty of the sin against the Holy Spirit will suffer eternal chastisement (Matt. 25:41, 46; Mark 9:48; Rev. 14:11, etc.).

IV. WHO CAN COMMIT THE SIN AGAINST THE HOLY SPIRIT?

By definition those who to the bitter end refuse to repent and accept the Saviour. But can it be that one of God's children, truly born again might commit such a sin? We believe that he cannot since he has already allowed himself to be convicted by the Holy Spirit who has entered into him. If that be so, what is the meaning of the following verses:

"For as touching those who were once enlightened and tasted of the heavenly gift, and were made partakers of the Holy Ghost, and tasted the good word of God, and the powers of the age to come, and then fell away, it is impossible to renew them again unto repentance" (Heb. 6:4-6). (Let it be noted straightaway that the expression translated as "were made partakers of the Holy Ghost" does not necessarily imply that mention is here being made of those who have been truly regenerated. It may be that a *partaker* experienced a deep conviction of sin and of righteousness which, however, his soul thrust aside.) Turn to Hebrews 10:29, also to Romans 8:13. "For if ye live after the flesh ye must die." (To a believer a life lived after the flesh implies resistance to the Holy Spirit who seeks to sanctify him; a continued opposition of this sort leads but to death.)

Such passages, we believe, have been written to remind us that man is always free to choose, even after his conversion, and that he must watch and endeavor to make constant progress. Even as God compels no unbeliever to become converted, even so does He not constrain those who call themselves believers to submit to sanctification. If they wish, they may live after the flesh, grieving the Spirit, whom they resist and perhaps even suppress. If they act thus and maintain such an attitude in the face of their claim to be born again, it is evident that they will be sinning against the Spirit, and their ultimate end will be eternal death. "For if, after they have escaped the defilements of the world, through the knowledge of the Lord and Saviour, Jesus Christ, they are again entangled therein and overcome, the last state is become worse with them than the first" (II Peter 2:20-22). If a man behave thus he would but show his insincerity and give proof that the work of regeneration had, in truth, never been completed within him. As in the case of the spies sent out by Moses, he will have traversed the Promised Land and tasted of its fruits but will have failed to take possession of them by faith (Num. 13:27-29; 14:36-38).

In contradistinction to this, however, we are convinced that a true child of God despite his stumblings, his weakness, his backsliding, will give proof of his uprightness of heart and the truth of his regeneration by returning faithfully to the Saviour, seeking sanctification anew. Let us summarize it: the sin against the Holy Spirit consists not of one or even many evil actions but of a deliberate abandoning of the Saviour combined with a resolute return to the former state of revolt and unbelief. This, a true Christian will never do; in striving to the very last he will be saved (Matt. 24:13) and the fountain of eternal life which has sprung up within him will never cease.

It is true, however, that certain Christians who have erred are haunted by the fear of having committed the unpardonable sin. They feel a sincere regret and constant grief; they desire greatly to return to the Saviour, but dare not since they are persuaded of their everlasting perdition. But we believe that their deep conviction of sin and their desire to return to the Saviour provide the very proof of the Spirit's work and continued presence within them. If they would but sincerely seek God's forgiveness, accepting it in faith, they would immediately find freedom, since Jesus has promised that He will in no wise cast out those who come unto Him (John 6:37).

There is the final question: May we think or say of anyone that he has committed the unforgivable sin? No, indeed, for the Lord alone knoweth them that are His (II Tim. 2:19) and it is not for us to judge them. Let us beware of so doing, seeking nevertheless, to warn those who are in sin, praying for them that they may escape such a terrible danger.

How, therefore, are we to understand the following passage: "If any man see his brother sinning a sin not unto death, he shall ask and God will give him life for them that sin not unto death. There is a sin unto death: not concerning this do I say that he should make request" (I John 5:16).

It would appear that this text is not connected with the sin against the Spirit, which a true "brother" would not commit. Rather, it speaks, we believe, of a sin serious enough to involve the physical death of that Christian who has committed it, and not of his spiritual perdition. Paul speaks of a similar instance when he says: "Deliver such a one unto Satan for the destruction of the flesh, that the spirit may be saved in the day of the Lord Jesus."

Also: "For this cause many among you are weak and sickly, and not a few sleep . . . But when we are judged, we are chastened of the Lord that we may not be condemned with the world" (I Cor. 11:30-32; 5:5). It follows therefore that we must watch ceaselessly and test ourselves lest we incur the Lord's punishment; and if we see a brother err, it is only by maintaining entire dependence upon God that we shall know how to intercede and act to restore him to repentance.

CONCLUSION

In the face of such solemn teaching, do we not feel an urgent need to examine our consciences? If we have not yet believed and still hear His voice today, may we tremble at the thought of hardening our hearts and hasten, before it be too late, to yield to the conviction which the Spirit brings. If we are already children of God, let us watch continually lest we turn back and fall prey again to worldly enticement. Let us search ourselves to know whether we seek that sanctification without which no man will see the Lord. But if, despite a sincere wish on our part to follow Christ, the adversary ceaselessly presents the bogey of fear of sinning against the Holy Spirit, may we grasp the shield of faith and recall to mind the promises of grace made to all those who wish to believe, not forgetting that if our heart condemn us "God is greater than our heart and knoweth all things" (I John 3:20).

Chapter 3

REGENERATION AND BAPTISM
OF THE HOLY SPIRIT

IN THIS AND THE FOLLOWING CHAPTERS we shall deal with the work of the Spirit in a heart which has yielded to a conviction of sin and accepted the Saviour. At the very moment of conversion the Holy Spirit, through the working of faith, brings about in such a heart the following operations which are but the differing aspects of one and the same intervention:

1. The Spirit regenerates the believer
2. The Spirit baptizes him
3. The believer receives the Spirit
4. The Spirit adopts him
5. He sets a seal upon him
6. He gives him the earnest of eternal salvation
7. The Spirit dwells within him
8. He anoints him for service

We shall study in succession these different actions, remembering the while that they are simultaneous and that they form the experience of a child of God as he stands upon the threshold of spiritual life. They are, as it were, the many facets of that royal gem which is the Spirit's gift, and each one enables us to understand a particular aspect of the Lord's work accomplished in us at the first moment of belief.

I. REGENERATION

1. What is regeneration?

From the spiritual point of view the soul of sinful man is dead and estranged from God, for the wages of sin is death

(Rom. 6:23). By the miracle of regeneration the soul is revived, newly begotten and granted eternal life. Jesus described this experience as being born anew (John 3:3, 7). It goes without saying that without this it is impossible for any man to be saved.

2. Who effects this regeneration?

"Except a man be born of water and the Spirit he cannot enter into the kingdom of God. That which is born of the flesh is flesh; and that which is born of the Spirit is spirit" (John 3:5, 6). It is the Holy Spirit who accomplishes this work. The flesh, that is our Self, counts for nothing; constant effort, good resolutions, good works, are completely insufficient. It is the Spirit who quickens, for the Almighty alone can effect the miracle of life (John 6:63). Paul speaks of regeneration in other terms of equal clearness: "Even when we were dead through our trespasses, [God] quickened us together with Christ . . . and raised us up with him and made us to sit with him in the heavenly places in Christ Jesus" (Eph. 2:5-6). He too attributes to the Spirit the life which quickens the believer: "If we live by the Spirit, by the Spirit let us also walk" (Gal. 5:25).

"Not by works done in righteousness, which we did ourselves, but according to his mercy he saved us, through the washing of regeneration and renewing of the Holy Ghost which he poured out upon us richly through Jesus Christ, our Saviour" (Titus 3:5-6). Our sinful soul, therefore, is not in need of *evolution* but of *revolution;* of spiritual resurrection. Do we still seek to "improve" ourselves—a laughable project for one who is dead—or are we already born anew?

3. When does regeneration take place?

At that very moment when the heart, under the Spirit's double conviction of sin and righteousness, accepts the Saviour, who is presented to him. On God's part it is an immediate act even though man may have taken years to reach the point of yielding and receiving salvation. "But to as many as received him [the Light, Jesus Christ], to them gave he the right to become the children of God, even to them that believe on his name: which were born not of blood, nor of the will of man, but of God" (John 1:12-13).

By means of new birth we receive life eternal; this grace is given us as soon as we believe: "He that believeth on the Son hath eternal life . . . He that believeth my word and believeth him that sent me, hath eternal life and cometh not into judgment, but hath passed out of death into life" (John 3:36; 5: 24).

Since regeneration is therefore both indispensable and immediate, if we have not already received it, why do we not grasp it now, through an act of faith? A conviction of sin would be useless were it not allied to the faith which lays hold of the life of the Spirit.

II. THE BAPTISM OF THE HOLY SPIRIT

In speaking of Jesus Christ, John the Baptist declared: "I baptized you with water; but he shall baptize you with the Holy Ghost" (Mark 1:8). This important statement is also to be found in the other three Gospels (Matt. 3:11; Luke 3: 16; John 1:33). Jesus Himself reiterated it when He enjoined His disciples not to leave Jerusalem, but rather to await that which the Father had promised, "which, said he, ye heard from me; for John indeed baptized with water; but ye shall be baptized with the Holy Ghost not many days hence" (Acts 1:4-5). This promise is explicit: Christ baptizes His children with the Holy Spirit and this baptism is essential to all true disciples. It is, therefore, essential that we should comprehend the nature of the Spirit's baptism and the way in which we may receive it.

1. The nature of the Holy Spirit's baptism.

This we shall endeavor to understand by confining ourselves strictly to the Biblical use of this term as revealed in the few passages which make mention of it. Confusion is always more readily avoided if we attribute to Biblical expressions no more than the strict meaning given to them by Scripture.

Our definition will be drawn from the most lucid text which the New Testament contains on this subject (I Cor. 12:13). "For in one Spirit we were all baptized into one body, whether Jews or Greeks whether bond or free; and were all made to drink of one Spirit." From this we can infer that the Spirit's baptism is the act whereby God makes us members of Christ's Body.

While discoursing beforehand to His disciples on the ministry of the Spirit, Jesus Christ said to them: "In that day ye shall know that I am in my Father, and ye in me and I in you" (John 14:20). It is by the very baptism of the Spirit that man, hitherto estranged from God, is placed (immersed) in Jesus Christ, receiving through faith this position in Him. From henceforth he is seated with Christ in the heavenly places (Eph. 2:6). This sovereign position becomes to the believer the source of life and the basis of victory. Paul's words, "For in one Spirit were we all baptized into one body," were addressed to the Corinthians whom the Apostle charges with being carnal and babes in Christ (I Cor. 12:13; 3:1-3). Here, then, is further proof that the baptism of the Spirit bears relation, not to the believer's spiritual state, but to his position. We can thus make our first definition more complete; the baptism of the Spirit is the act whereby God gives to the believer his position in Jesus Christ. (The passages in Gal. 3:27 and Rom. 6:3-4, which we have yet to study, lead us to the same conclusion.)

The cardinal importance of such an act becomes apparent when it is borne in mind that well over a hundred passages in the New Testament underline the fact that a child of God is "in Christ." All that we subsequently become and receive springs from that position in Christ, which the Spirit's baptism confers upon us.

It has already been pointed out that the baptism of the Spirit is not mentioned as affecting Jesus Christ. When He was baptized in the River Jordan, He was filled with the Holy Spirit, invested with the power of the Spirit, anointed by the Holy Ghost, according to the expressions used by Luke 3:22; 4:1, 14, 18; but nowhere is it said that He was baptized of the Holy Spirit, though many of the Spirit's workings are mentioned in connection with Christ. Since the baptism of the Spirit is linked with the believer's position in Christ, how, indeed, could the Saviour have been immersed in Himself or united to His own Body?

Further on we shall see that God does not remain satisfied with merely placing us "in Christ"; He, at the same time, places Christ "within us" through the Spirit. His presence in our hearts enables us to carry into effect in our daily life all that, in principle, the Spirit's baptism has conferred on us. In other words, this baptism places us in Jesus Christ and enfolds us in His Grace, while the presence and fullness of the Spirit put Christ within us, making us possessors of all His riches.

Note that the definition of the baptism of the Spirit, drawn from I Corinthians 12:13 harmonizes with the only two historical examples of such an experience, given us in the New Testament.

According to Acts 1:5 the company of one hundred and twenty were baptized with the Holy Spirit on the day of Pentecost and became members of the Body of Christ created on that day by the Spirit.

The Gentiles, in Cornelius' house were also baptized with the Spirit at the very moment in which they became through faith members of that same Body (Acts 11:15-16).

2. There is but one spiritual baptism.

The following different expressions are used in the Scriptures:

"Baptized with the Holy Ghost" (Acts 1:5).

"Baptized into Christ" (Gal. 3:27; Rom. 6:3).

"Baptized into his death" (Rom. 6:3).

Must we therefore conclude that, besides the baptism of water there are three different baptisms of the Spirit which must be received one after the other? This is not so, because the writer of the Epistle to the Ephesians, in laying down the Church's spiritual basis, states explicitly that "There is . . . one baptism" (Eph. 4:4-6). It is, moreover, quite clear that these three expressions have but one meaning since it is the Spirit who, by immersing us in Jesus Christ, causes us to die to Self that we may live anew with Him.

3. At what stage do we receive the baptism of the Spirit?

Since the Spirit's baptism makes us members of the Body of Christ, there can be no doubt that we receive it when we turn to the Saviour and accept Him. The experience of the hundred and twenty disciples at Pentecost cannot in all points be compared with our experience since they belonged to two different dispensations. Nevertheless they received the baptism of the Spirit at the moment of entry into the Church and the new dispensation. The case of the heathen at Cornelius' house is still more striking since, in this connection, it is comparable to ours; they were baptized with the Spirit immediately upon their conversion to Christianity, and they became regenerated (Acts 10:44; 11:15-16). The baptism of the Spirit and regeneration are, therefore, effected simultaneously. In truth, as soon as I am in Christ through faith, Christ is also in me to give me life by new birth.

Note furthermore that conversion and regeneration are also simultaneous since they are two aspects of one experience. Conversion is the action of a man who abandons sin and turns toward God; regeneration is God's miracle whereby he receives eternal life; these two actions take place at the same time, for the man who is sincere in his belief is immediately regenerated (John 5:24).

Herein lies the reason for the absence of any text in Scripture urging believers to seek for the Spirit's baptism. Being, indeed, already in Christ, how shall they search for what they received at the outset of their Christian life? In this connection note that in all the texts wherein Paul speaks to Christians about the baptism of the Spirit, the verb used is in the past tense because experience of it has already been made: "in one Spirit all of us . . . were baptized" (I Cor. 12:13 Wey.). "Having been buried with him in baptism wherein ye were also raised with him" (Col. 2:12). "For as many of you as were baptized into Christ did put on Christ" (Gal. 3:27). (See also Rom. 6:3-4.)

It is true that, at the present day, many people give the name of "baptism of the Spirit" to an experience taking place after regeneration. But if what has been written about the experience given to the early disciples (see pages 38-40) is borne in mind, and if reference is made to all those passages which apply to post-Pentecost believers, and wherein the words "the baptism of the Holy Ghost" occur, it will be seen that not one of these will supply sufficient ground to justify such a conception which, to a large extent, is the result of a confusion of terms. That experience which it is possible and expedient to possess after regeneration is called in the Bible not the baptism of the Holy Ghost but the fullness of the Holy Spirit (see chapter on the Fullness of the Holy Spirit).

4. In what way is the baptism of the Spirit received?

Since the baptism of the Spirit gives us our position in Christ and makes us members of His Body, it is clear that we receive it quite simply *by faith:* "having been buried with him in baptism, wherein ye were also raised with him through faith in the working of God" (Col. 2:12). (This text deals, beyond all question, with the baptism of the Spirit, since baptism by water alone cannot result in our spiritual resurrection.) And John writes: "Whosoever shall confess that Jesus is the Son of God, God abideth in him, and he in God" (I John 4:15). Man, therefore, receives his position in God and in Christ by the very fact of believing and confessing the Saviour's name.

Consequently if you have not passed through the essential

experience of the Spirit's baptism you need not await it, plead or fight to obtain it. Come to God for salvation, believing in Jesus Christ and His promise to baptize His own with His Spirit, and you will receive it.

5. Is the baptism of the Spirit for all men?

Many persons think that the baptism of the Spirit is a special experience reserved for certain privileged people, and a few of God's greatest servants. This is not so and the Bible teaches that this grace is open to all believers. The very evidence of this is seen when we realize that without it we are neither saved nor made members of Christ's Body. Note the word *all* in the following passages: "For in one Spirit we are *all* baptized into one body, whether Jews or Greeks, whether bond or free; [that is to say each one without exception], and were *all* made to drink of one Spirit" (I Cor. 12:13). "For ye are all sons of God, through faith in Jesus Christ. For as many of you [i.e., all] as were baptized into Christ did put on Christ" (Gal. 3:26-27). The Saviour Himself gave an unqualified assurance that He would baptize His disciples with the Spirit as He was to make all of them His witnesses (Acts 1:5, 8). In fact, John the Baptist, in announcing Him who was to deliver the world from sin and baptize with the Holy Ghost, presented these two actions as being the one as universal as the other (John 1:29, 33).

Consequently this experience is both necessary and open to you.

6. What are the results of the Spirit's baptism?

a. It makes us members of the Body of Christ (I Cor. 12:13) as has been already explained. Henceforth we take part in His life and His Work.

b. It enables us to put on Christ. "For as many of you as were baptized into Christ did put on Christ" (Gal. 3:27). The believer, immersed through baptism in Christ, is enveloped by Him and thus puts on Christ; or in other words, receives the new nature. (Without any doubt, this text implies that the

Spirit's baptism and baptism "into Christ" are identical; no reference can here be intended to baptism by water which, of itself, would be insufficient to clothe us with the new nature.)

The child of God bears within himself the new man (Col. 3:10-11); being in Christ he is a new creature and the old things are passed away. Thus all things have become new (II Cor. 5:17).

c. It causes us to die and be raised again with Christ. "Having been buried with him in baptism, wherein ye were also raised with him through faith" (Col. 2:12).

"We were buried therefore with him through baptism into death: that like as Christ was raised from the dead . . . so we also might walk in newness of life" (Rom. 6:4). If I, through the Spirit, am given a place in Christ, it is plain that I must lose my own life and receive His. What magnificent results attend upon the baptism of the Spirit, and what folly it would be on my part to remain in ignorance of them!

Let us again note that these two passages, Colossians 2:12 and Romans 6:4, do not contain the complete expression, "the baptism of the Spirit," but only the words "with him in baptism" and "baptism into death." In both cases, however, the result comprises death and spiritual resurrection with Christ. As it was remarked in connection with Galatians 3:27, baptism by water could not have such an effect. These verses are therefore primarily concerned with the baptism of the Spirit. Further on we shall see what connection exists between the two baptisms.

Note how certain results of the Spirit's baptism can be allied to those coming from regeneration. This serves to show the close relationship that exists between these two experiences which take effect simultaneously.

d. Lastly, the Spirit's baptism creates unity among the children of God.

"For in one Spirit were we all baptized into one body, whether Jews or Greeks, whether bond or free" (I Cor. 12:

13). "For as many of you as were baptized into Christ did put on Christ. There can be neither Jew nor Greek, there can be neither bond nor free, there can be no male and female: for ye are all one man in Christ Jesus" (Gal. 3:27-28).

By becoming members of one Body we are united not only to the Head but also one to another. Wherefore Paul beseeches us "to keep the unity of the Spirit in the bond of peace," and this appeal he bases on the fact that there is one body, one Spirit, one baptism (Eph. 4:3, 6).

Let us thank God that He has created unity among His own children, but may we be humbled by the remembrance that we have so frequently disrupted this harmony and hindered its manifestation.

7. Does not the baptism of the Spirit result in investing us with power, as in Acts 1:5-8?

It is clear that the act of reception of the Spirit, at the time of baptism, places within us the source of power. Nevertheless Scripture teaches us quite plainly that, unfortunately, it is possible to be baptized with the Spirit and to possess His presence within us and yet to lack any manifestation of His power because we grieve Him. Here are two examples:

a. The Corinthians were all baptized with the Holy Ghost (I Cor. 12:13); they were the temple of the Spirit who lived within them (6:19); yet they remained carnal, spiritually still in childhood and unable to take anything stronger than milk (3:1-3). They were not clothed with power.

b. The Galatians were also sons of God; they had all been baptized into Christ and had put on Christ (Gal. 3:26-27). Despite this, Paul taxes them with turning away from the Gospel (1:6), with returning to "weak and beggarly rudiments" (4:9), and he fears lest he should have labored for them in vain. The Spirit's baptism is, therefore, not always followed by a manifestation of power. We have just seen that it is not enough that the soul be baptized; it must also be filled with the Spirit. Then, indeed, can power be manifested both within and around it. At Pentecost the one hundred and twenty disciples were not only baptized with the Spirit (Acts 1:5), but were also filled by Him (Acts 2:4). Herein lies the reason for the extraordinary and sudden effectiveness of their ministry.

8. Is it imperative that certain outward manifestations should accompany the Spirit's baptism?

In the epistles which form the statement of all Christian doctrine we find no text which makes mention of this. In the Acts of the Apostles the phrase "baptism of the Spirit" is twice followed by the ability to speak with tongues.

Acts 1:5 and 2:4 in the case of the one hundred and twenty at Pentecost.

Acts 10:46 and 11:15, 16 in the case of the Gentiles at Cornelius' house. However, in both instances it was indispensable that there should be some exterior sign; had there been none, the disciples would not have known that the Spirit had fallen upon them, nor that the heathen could receive the same blessing. For us, who live after that introductory period of the new dispensation, there is no passage in Scripture which inevitably links the gift of tongues with baptism of the Spirit. On the contrary, Paul, when he asserts that *all* are baptized with the Spirit, distinctly states that all do not speak with tongues (I Cor. 12:13, 30). (See page 193.)

As to the quakings, the cries, the trembling, the very contortions which might accompany the baptism of the Spirit, of these the Bible does not speak, but solemnly avers that God is a God of peace, good order and seemliness, besides holiness (I Cor. 14:33, 40). If such things do come about, their origin is not from above.

9. Is there any connection between baptism by water and baptism of the Spirit?

Yes, indeed, there is! Just as the baptism of the Spirit is the act of immersion in Christ, of death and spiritual resurrection with Him to become a member of His Body, even so baptism by water is the symbol, the outward demonstration of the

Spirit's action in the believer's heart. But no claim can be made asserting the impossibility of receiving the baptism of the Spirit without first undergoing baptism by water through immersion. If this point is of special interest compare the following passages (Rom. 6:3-4; Col. 2:12; John 3:5; Acts 8:36, 39; 10:47).

Let us not leave this subject without putting to our own selves this definite question: "Have I been baptized with the Holy Spirit?" Should the answer be *No,* may we become baptized through faith without further delay by coming to Christ for salvation.

CHAPTER 4

THE RECEIVING OF THE HOLY SPIRIT

PAUL DECLARES that "if any man hath not the Spirit of Christ, he is none of His" (Rom. 8:9). It is therefore imperative that we should know not only whether we are already regenerated and baptized of the Spirit, but also whether His presence is within us at the present moment.

I. THE PROMISES RELATING TO THE RECEIVING OF THE SPIRIT

They are both numerous and explicit. Attention has already been drawn to several in the Old Testament (see pages 34, 35). The Lord Jesus Christ, quoting them, enlarges upon them: "And I will pray the Father and he shall give you another Comforter that he may be with you forever, even the Spirit of truth" (John 14:16). "It is expedient for you that I go away: for if I go not away the Comforter will not come unto you; but if I go, I will send him unto you" (John 16:7). "But ye shall receive power, when the Holy Ghost is come upon you: and ye shall be my witnesses" (Acts 1:8). Peter, also, made special reference to this matter: "Ye shall receive the gift of the Holy Ghost. For to you is the promise, and to your children, and to all that are afar off, even as many as the Lord our God shall call unto him" (Acts 2:38, 39). In the face of such promises, besides all those that are to be found elsewhere in Scripture, no truly believing soul can doubt that the Holy Spirit is for him also.

II. HOW DO WE RECEIVE THE SPIRIT?

This question has posed to the believer many problems which require us to dwell, first of all, on what is not indispensable in connection with receiving the Spirit, before mention is made of the one thing that is necessary.

1. Those things on which the receiving of the Spirit is not dependent.

a. Must there be a period of waiting before receiving the Spirit? Paul states in Galatians 3:13-14 that "Christ redeemed us from the curse of the law . . . that we might receive the promise of the Spirit *through faith*." If, therefore, the Spirit is received through faith it is quite unnecessary for the believer to spend months and even years awaiting Him. Paul remarks on this to the Ephesians: "having also believed ye were sealed with the Holy Spirit of promise" (Eph. 1:13).

The Book of Acts, however, would seem to indicate that some men believed but did not immediately receive the Spirit. Let us see who these persons were:

1) The disciples before Pentecost.

To the assembly of His disciples, Jesus Christ charges that they should not move away from Jerusalem but that they should await the fulfillment of the Father's promise. This period of waiting lasted ten days and was spent in prayer (Acts 1:14).

Why did these one hundred and twenty have to wait? Because the time appointed by God for the outpouring of the Holy Spirit had not yet arrived. For us, who have come after Pentecost it is not the same.

2) The Samaritans.

The Samaritans believed and were baptized, nevertheless they did not receive the Spirit until later, following the apostles' intervention (Acts 8:12, 15-17). What is the explanation for this? It would appear that it lies in this: it should never be forgotten that the Book of Acts does not constitute a statement of doctrine and that constant reference is made to people whose circumstances differed from ours, as, for example the disciples before Pentecost and the Samaritans.

Who were these Samaritans? A pagan race despised by the Jews, and in whose religion there existed but a slight shade of Judaism. Jesus Himself, when sending out His disciples, had forbidden them to enter into Samaritan towns (Matt. 10:5); moreover James and John had expressed a desire that fire might fall from Heaven and consume one of their townships (Luke 9:54). A big gap had, therefore, to be bridged. In Acts 8 the door of the Gospel had not yet been opened to the Gentiles and not until later in chapter 10 was free access given to them. Peter, to whom the Lord had entrusted the keys of the kingdom, used them to open the door to the Jews at Pentecost and to the Gentiles in Cornelius' house. Thus the Samaritans occupied an intermediary position. Hitherto the Spirit had been given only to the Jews; it is not surprising, therefore, that direct intervention by the apostles, especially Peter, was necessary before the Samaritans also could receive Him.

3) The disciples at Ephesus.

Paul meets twelve disciples and asks them this celebrated question, "Did ye receive the Holy Spirit when ye believed?" (Acts 19:1-7). Whence the conclusion has frequently been drawn that it was possible to believe and yet fail to receive the Spirit.

But give closer study to this conversation. Those disciples knew nothing of the Spirit and had received only the baptism of John the Baptist; Paul then told them that they had only experienced repentance (v. 4). Indeed thousands of Jews who had received the Forerunner's baptism had not been regenerated by it, for repentance and confession of sins are but the very first steps toward salvation. These must be followed by faith in Jesus. Hitherto the twelve disciples at Ephesus had lacked this faith, but as soon as they accepted the Saviour and were baptized in His name, then, without delay, they received the Holy Spirit. Note, besides, that Paul did not ask them if they had received the Holy Spirit *since* they had believed but "when ye believed." This well proves the rule that the Spirit is received at the very first moment of belief.

Moreover, whatever explanation may be given for these three instances here quoted, it is evident that a great number of other Christians mentioned in the Acts received the Spirit without having to submit to any delay.

(As to Saul, we do not know whether he was truly converted before or after those three days spent in darkness at Damascus [Acts 9:9], nor if he received the Spirit before being filled with the Spirit [v. 17].) In this connection we shall confine ourselves to the mention of the three thousand in Acts 2:41 and the Gentiles at Cornelius' house (10:44). So little had the latter to wait that Peter did not even have time to conclude his address.

Lastly, a more telling fact is that the epistles (which form the charter of the Christian life) give no grounds for saying that the believer must needs wait to receive the Spirit. Indeed, further study will show that their teaching is contrary to this.

2. Is there any need to pray at length to receive the Spirit?

Jesus did, indeed, declare: "If ye then being evil know how to give good gifts unto your children, how much more shall your heavenly Father give the Holy Spirit to them that ask Him?" (Luke 11:13). He also said: "All things whatsoever ye pray and ask for, believe that ye have received them, and ye shall have them" (Mark 11:24).

If the one hundred and twenty in the Upper Room passed ten days in prayer (Acts 1:14), it was, as has been previously remarked, because the moment decided upon by God for the Spirit's descent had not yet arrived. In the same manner the prayer made by Peter and John on behalf of the Samaritans (Acts 8:15) can be explained by the fact that before the event in Cornelius' house, the Spirit had not yet fallen upon the Gentiles.

We can, therefore, infer that if those who are unconverted

are urged to ask for the gift of the Spirit, no passage in Scripture imposes upon them the condition of striving in prayer to obtain it. It is the same as receiving pardon. God tells us to ask for it and to take it straightway through faith. Man might strive vainly over many years in prayer to achieve purification from his sins, but he will only possess the assurance of salvation when, after asking for it, he ceases to strive and accepts through faith what God had long before bestowed upon him in principle. Paul states that "Christ redeemed us . . . that we might receive the promise of the Spirit *through faith*" (Gal. 3:13-14).

If, therefore, we are not yet born anew, let us ask of God the Spirit whom He has shed abroad once and forever; then, ceasing to ask may we receive Him immediately by faith, expressing our gratitude for this wonderful gift. On the other hand, if we are children of God let us not seek after a favor which we already possess, for without the Spirit no man belongs to Him (Rom. 8:9).

3. Is the laying on of hands indispensable for the receiving of the Spirit?

Here again no text in the epistles authorizes the obligation of the laying on of hands before the Spirit can be received. And in the whole of the Acts only three instances in this connection claim our attention. (These are nearly always the same cases.)

a. The Samaritans received the Holy Spirit through the laying on of the apostles' hands (Acts 8:17-18). It has already been remarked that this direct intervention by Peter and John can only be explained by the fact that the door of the Gospel had hitherto not been opened to heathen races.

b. Saul of Tarsus experienced the laying on of hands by Ananias who said to him: "The Lord . . . hath sent me that thou mayest receive thy sight and be filled with the Holy Ghost" (Acts 9:17). But in verse 12 the Lord said of this same Saul, "he hath seen a man . . . laying his hands on him that he might receive his sight." It would appear, therefore, that the laying on of hands in this instance was connected, not with the Holy Spirit, but with healing.

c. Lastly, the disciples at Ephesus received the Spirit "when Paul had laid his hands upon them" (Acts 19:6). These were the only believers in the Book of the Acts who, coming after Pentecost and Cornelius, received the Spirit in this manner. It is obvious that no compulsory rule can be drawn from this example of twelve men nor can it be said to Christians "without the laying on of hands you cannot receive the Spirit." On the contrary all other instances in the Book of Acts reveal that the rule consists of receiving the Holy Spirit without any intermediary; take, for example, the one hundred and twenty in the Upper Room (Acts 2:4), the three thousand on the day of Pentecost (2:38), the Gentiles at Cornelius' house (10:44), the disciples at Antioch in Pisidia (13:48, 52) without mentioning all those who simply believed and consequently received the divine gift. Moreover, it is clear that, if the laying on of hands had been indispensable, neither the one hundred and twenty nor the Gentiles with Cornelius would have received the Spirit.

In connection with this matter, mention of the laying on of hands is made in I Timothy 4:14: "Neglect not the gift that is in thee, which was given thee by prophecy, with the laying on of the hands of the presbytery"; and further on in II Timothy 1:6, "I put thee in remembrance that thou stir up the gift of God which is in thee through the laying on of my hands." It might be questioned whether Paul alludes, in these two passages to the general gift of the Spirit; it would seem in the former text more especially, that the Apostle is speaking of a spiritual gift of value for the ministry rather than of Timothy's receiving of the Spirit.

The Acts also provides us with examples of the laying on of hands in connection with the ministry: on the deacons (6:

6) then on Barnabas and Saul (13:3). But this is a different matter.

To summarize: the laying on of hands is Biblical and God may, by this means, convey to us some grace or gift, but it is never indispensable nor does it enter into the experience of every Christian.

4. Is the gift of tongues a necessary proof of the reception of the Spirit?

Many have asked themselves this question in face of the repeated occasions in the Acts when such a gift accompanied reception of the Spirit. Let us examine these instances of the gift of tongues as quoted in Acts and let us ask ourselves whether they establish a valid rule for us. These instances are three in number:

a. The one hundred and twenty in the Upper Room were all filled with the Spirit and started to talk in other tongues (Acts 2:1-4).

Note that God gave them three external signs: the sound as of a mighty wind which filled the house, tongues of fire which rested over each one, and, lastly, unknown but understandable tongues (vv. 8, 11). Why were all these signs necessary? To prove that the promise had been accomplished and that the Spirit had been given to them. Without these signs the disciples would not have dared to believe that the new dispensation had commenced. We stand in a very different situation; by the New Testament and the experience of the Church we know that the Spirit has been spread abroad in accordance with the promise given. No one would dream of claiming the signs of a mighty wind and of tongues of fire experienced by the one hundred and twenty. Similarly this single example at Pentecost provides us with no authorization to claim for all the gift of tongues.

b. The Gentiles with Cornelius, while Peter was still speaking, received the Spirit and started to speak with tongues (Acts 10:44-46). There again, an external sign was absolutely necessary; without this sign, Peter and the converted Jews who accompanied him, would not have believed that the gift of the Spirit had also been granted to pagan races. Faced with the astonishment of the circumcised faithful, Peter then cried aloud: "Can any man forbid the water that these should not be baptized which have received the Holy Ghost as well as we?" (10:45, 47).

There is suspicion that, had this sign of the gift of tongues not been given, the disciples would have refused to baptize the Gentiles and admit them into the Church. As for us, we have no need of this external sign to know that we, of pagan race, are admitted into the Church and that the Spirit has been granted to us also. In no wise, therefore, does this passage impose upon us the obligation of receiving the gift of tongues.

c. Lastly, the disciples at Ephesus spoke with tongues after receiving the Spirit (Acts 19:6). They were in the same situation in which we find ourselves today, coming after Pentecost and Cornelius. Their example goes to show quite simply that God in His sovereignty can grant the gift of tongues to whomsoever He desires. But in view of the thousands of believers (mentioned in the Acts) who never spoke with tongues, the instance of twelve men cannot alone constitute the necessity for Christians the world over to speak with tongues as a proof of having received the Spirit.

What we learn in this connection from the Acts is fully confirmed by the epistles, or rather by the only epistle which deals with this subject, I Corinthians. On two occasions Paul declares that the gift of tongues is not given to all; the Spirit gives, as He wishes, to each one a special gift; one gift to one man and another to his fellow creature. Also all do not speak with tongues (I Cor. 12:8-11, 28-30). (The study of this subject will be completed in the chapter dealing with the gifts of the Spirit.)

5. Must baptism by water necessarily precede the reception of the Spirit?

To the crowd which listened to him on the day of Pentecost Peter declared: "Repent ye and be baptized every one of you in the name of Jesus Christ, unto the remission of your sins" (Acts 2:38). This has prompted the question of whether God's ordering of the Christian path is as follows:

Repentance
Baptism by water
The receiving of the Holy Spirit

A yet closer examination of the Book of Acts taken as a whole makes it possible to state that the cases in which the receiving of the Spirit is consequent upon baptism form the exception. They are confined to three:

a. The three thousand at Pentecost already mentioned (2: 38). These men belonged to the number of those who had rejected and crucified Jesus (v. 23). It is, therefore, hardly surprising that Peter asked them first of all to acknowledge publicly by baptism that their attitude toward Jesus had changed and that they now believed on Him whom they had put to a criminal's death. In doing this they would receive the Holy Spirit.

Peter speaks in a different vein when addressing the Gentiles at Cornelius' house. These people had never before adopted an antagonistic attitude toward Him. Thus Peter stresses only the need of faith: "To him bear all the prophets witness that through his name every one that believeth on Him shall receive remission of sins" (10:43). On hearing these words, Cornelius and his friends believed and immediately received the Spirit (v. 44). Had the receiving of the Spirit by them depended on the preliminary administration of baptism by water, there is no doubt that they would never have received the Spirit. Indeed, even Peter intimates that he would have refused them baptism by water (10:47), while the faithful at Jerusalem reproach him for having even entered among the pagans and were only quieted after many explanations (11:2-3, 18).

b. The Samaritans first believed, were baptized and then

later received the Spirit (vv. 8:12, 17). It has already been pointed out that this case had a unique quality since it concerned a semi-pagan people who were admitted into the Church prior to the outpouring of the Spirit upon the Gentiles at Cornelius' house. Thus their experience proves no pertinent guide for us.

c. Lastly, the twelve disciples at Ephesus were first baptized and then received the Spirit (19:5-6).

An endeavor has been made to provide several explanations of this instance, but irrespective of the one which is accepted it must be stressed yet again that the experience of these twelve persons standing alone, as it does, in the Book of Acts cannot establish a binding precedent for all believers.

Furthermore the truth of this is clearly upheld by the fact that other instances of baptism mentioned in the Acts reveal that faith (and the consequent reception of the Spirit) precedes rather than follows baptism. Philip said to the eunuch, "If thou believest with all thine heart thou mayest [be baptized]" (Acts 8:37); Saul not only received but was also filled by the Spirit before his baptism (Acts 9:17-18). Lydia believed before being baptized, as indeed did the gaoler at Philippi (Acts 16:14-15, 31). For it is written: "Whosoever shall confess that Jesus is the Son of God, God abideth in him, and he in God" (I John 4:15); consequently all these persons mentioned received the Spirit prior to baptism by water—such a baptism (despite its significance and value) is not, therefore, one of the conditions under which we receive the Spirit.

A period of delay, prolonged prayer, the laying on of hands, the gift of tongues and baptism by water, though they are all mentioned in Scripture in connection with specific instances, are not indispensable stipulations relating to the receiving of the Spirit. In this way God reveals His desire to save the just *by faith* without binding the granting of spiritual grace to a necessary action, rite or external sign of any sort. May we bear in mind that "This is the work of God that ye believe on him," and let us hasten to fulfill the only condition that He Himself imposes upon us.

6. Faith the only necessary condition for the receiving of the Spirit.

So numerous are the passages which testify to this great truth that we shall endeavor to classify them in different groups.

a. The Spirit is given to him that believes.

Jesus exclaimed: "He that believeth on me, . . . out of his belly shall flow rivers of living water"; and John adds, "This spake he of the Spirit which they that believed on him were to receive" (John 7:38-39). Paul, speaking to the Ephesians said, "In whom [Christ], having also *believed* ye were sealed with the Holy Spirit of promise," and then he prays to God that they may be "strengthened with power through His Spirit in the inward man; that Christ may dwell in your hearts through *faith*" (Eph. 1:13; 3:16-17). It is, therefore, by faith that Christ comes into our hearts through the Spirit.

The Galatians who had accepted salvation through faith ran the risk of falling back under the law and of securing their salvation through works. To them also the apostle writes: "Received ye the Spirit by the works of the law or by the hearing of faith? . . . He, therefore, that supplieth to you the Spirit . . . doeth he it by the works of the law or by the hearing of faith?" (Gal. 3:2, 5). Clearly it was by faith alone that the Galatians had received the gift of God. An attempt to obtain or retain it by works of the law, by rites and external signs would make them "perfected in the flesh" (v. 3). In truth "Christ redeemed us from the curse of the law [and the works of the law] (v. 10) . . . that we might receive the promise of the Spirit *through faith*" (Gal. 3:13, 14).

Similarly when Paul listed for the Romans the fruits of justification *by faith* he writes of "the Holy Ghost which was given unto us" (Rom. 5:5). Lastly Peter declared that the one hundred and twenty disciples at Pentecost received the Holy Spirit through faith when he says of the Gentiles at Cornelius' house,

"God gave unto them the like gift as he did also unto us when we *believed* on the Lord Jesus Christ" (Acts 11:17). Confirming this, further on, he says "God ... bare them [the Gentiles] witness, giving them the Holy Ghost even as he did unto us; and he made no distinction between us and them, cleansing their hearts by faith" (Acts 15:8, 9).

b. The Spirit is given to him who obeys.

The apostles announced before the Sanhedrin, "We are witnesses of these things; and so is the Holy Ghost whom God hath given to them that obey him" (Acts 5:32).

What are God's primary instructions to us? "This is His commandment, that we should believe in the name of His Son Jesus Christ, and love one another" (I John 3:23). "This is the work of God, that ye believe on him whom he hath sent" (John 6:29). Paul also remarks that he received his apostleship "unto obedience of faith among all nations" (Rom. 1:5). Thus he who obeys is the same as he who believes, and naturally once he has received the Spirit he will perform the works of faith.

c. The Spirit is a gift which must be accepted.

Six times in the Acts is the Spirit called the "gift of God," given to those who obey and believe (2:38; 5:32; 8:20; 10:45; 11:17; 15:8).

What must be done to gain possession of a "gift" already made, for the Spirit has been poured forth upon all flesh since Pentecost? (Acts 2:17). Simply accept it, that is to say take it through faith. Fighting, prayer, waiting, accomplishing one rite or another—all these will never replace that definite act of faith which God asks of us.

It is precisely the same with that other "gift of God" which is eternal life (Rom. 6:23). Nothing in the world apart from faith will help us to receive it, but as soon as we believe we possess eternal life and receive the Spirit.

d. The Spirit is given to all who accept the Saviour.

Paul affirms that "he that is joined unto the Lord is one

spirit" and adds that "no man can say Jesus is Lord but in the Holy Spirit" (I Cor. 6:17; 12:3). From the moment when we acknowledge that Jesus is the Son of God, God dwells in us and we in God; and we know that He dwells in us through the Spirit whom He has given us (I John 4:15; 3:24). What a wonderful privilege!

Finally Jesus Himself declares, "Behold I stand at the door and knock; if any man hear my voice and open the door I will come in to him and will sup with him and he with me" (Rev. 3:20). But how may He enter into us? Clearly, only through the Spirit.

e. The Spirit is given to all who become the children of God.

We have just seen that without the Holy Spirit no one can say, "Jesus is Lord." Paul goes as far as to say, "If any man hath not the Spirit of Christ, he is none of his" (Rom. 8:9). (The Spirit of Christ is the Holy Spirit, since there is but one Spirit and the three persons of the Trinity are one.) Part I, Chapter 2, Point V.

It is therefore impossible to be a true Christian, to belong to the Lord without possessing the Holy Spirit. But the converse is equally true: all those who are children of God by new birth have the Holy Spirit.

Furthermore, how do we become the children of God? By the Spirit. "For as many as are led by the Spirit of God, these are sons of God" (Rom. 8:14). The assurance of salvation also comes to us through the Spirit who has been given unto us: "For ye received not the spirit of bondage again unto fear [fear of punishment, death and judgment]; but ye received the spirit of adoption whereby we cry Abba, Father. The Spirit himself beareth witness with our spirit that we are children of God" (Rom. 8:15, 16).

Thus, without Him we have neither assurance nor possession of eternal life. And lastly, here is a text from Galatians 4:4-7, "God sent forth his Son . . . that we might receive the adoption of sons. And because ye are sons, God sent forth the Spirit of his Son into our hearts crying Abba, Father. So that thou art no longer a bond-servant but a son."

It is beyond all question that we become sons of God through faith: "Whosoever believeth that Jesus is the Christ is begotten of God" (I John 5:1). Consequently it is also through faith at the moment of rebirth that we receive the Spirit. There are doubtless other passages which might be quoted in this connection but it would appear that the foregoing is sufficiently conclusive.

CONCLUSION

Let us thank God for placing within reach of all, both the gift of the Holy Spirit and the gift of His Son, while imposing no other condition but that of the exercise of faith. Then let us ask ourselves, relying on the Scriptures and not on our own feelings, whether indeed we have the Spirit. If we lack such an assurance, before continuing any further, shall we not believe and appropriate the grace which God offers us?

CHAPTER 5

ADOPTION AND THE CERTAINTY
OF SALVATION

I. ADOPTION BY THE SPIRIT

BY REASON OF THEIR SIN, all men created by God have
become sons of the Devil. Jesus declared as much to the
Jews although they were so religious and boasted of possessing
Abraham and God as their father, "Ye are of your father the
devil, and the lusts of your father it is your will to do" (John
8:44). And John adds that "he that doeth sin is of the devil"
and that "the whole world lieth in the evil one" (I John 3:8;
5:19). In consequence God is not the Father of all men as
many wrongly imagine and those who are unconverted cannot
say: "*Our* Father, who art in heaven." For them God is only
the Creator and shall shortly become the judge. He is the
Father only of those who through the Spirit have become His
children by adoption. What is adoption? It is entrance into a
new family. I was born a sinner in the Devil's family. Through
Christ I leave and enter the rich and exalted family of God. I
receive a new life, a new name, a new Father, new brothers and
sisters and a wonderful inheritance. Let us quote once again
those passages which we have already mentioned in connection
with the reception of the Spirit: "Ye received not the spirit of
bondage again unto fear; but ye received the Spirit of adoption
whereby we cry Abba, Father" (Rom. 8:15). "God sent forth
his Son . . . that we might receive the adoption of sons. And
because ye are sons, God sent forth the Spirit of his Son into
our hearts crying, Abba, Father" (Gal. 4:4, 6).

94

When extending pardon to us, God could have been content to treat us as pardoned servants, remote from Him as the created being is in relation to his Creator. But, "Behold what manner of love the Father hath bestowed upon us, that we should be called children of God!" And such we are through His Spirit (I John 3:1). Never can we render sufficient thanks for His wonderful salvation.

II. THE CERTAINTY OF SALVATION

Can it be possible for us, while here below, to have the certainty of salvation? To some such a claim denotes a certain arrogance; others believe that this certainty will come only after crossing the "eschatological line," that is to say on Christ's return or after death; lastly, some would wish to possess this certainty but only achieve a vague and distant hope. But what does the Bible say? It teaches that the certainty of salvation given to the believer rests upon two immovable pillars.

1. The written testimony of the Holy Spirit—the Word of God.

Scripture is full of promises such as this: "He that believeth on the Son hath eternal life" (John 3:36); and again, "These things have I written unto you that ye may know that ye *have* eternal life, even unto you that believe on the name of the Son of God" (I John 5:13). The Bible is the work of the Spirit and it is He who, by means of the prophets and the apostles, teaches us the way of salvation. Having twice stated that the Spirit testifies of Jesus Christ, John goes on to explain the nature of this testimony originating from God: "And the witness is this, that God gave unto us eternal life and this life is in his Son. He that hath the Son hath life" (I John 5:6-7; 11:12).

This forthright teaching reaches us through the Word of God; he who places his faith in Jesus Christ, if he draws his support not from his feelings but only from what is written, will have the assurance of life eternal.

2. The inner witness of the Holy Spirit.

Certainty of salvation based primarily and solely on faith in the Bible will find its confirmation in the heart through the Spirit. "For ye received not the spirit of bondage again unto fear; but ye received the spirit of adoption whereby we cry, Abba, Father. The Spirit himself beareth witness with our Spirit that we are children of God" (Rom. 8:15-16). Thus the Spirit is given to us to remove the constant fear of death and punishment, and to impart to us the certainty of our divine adoption and of life eternal. A denial of such certainty brushes aside simultaneously the witness of Scripture and that of the Spirit.

Several Biblical expressions add yet further confirmation of this Christian assurance. They have already been dwelt upon when speaking of the symbols of the Spirit (see page 20 ff.). To the Ephesians, Paul says, "In whom, having also believed ye were *sealed* with the Holy Spirit of promise, which is an *earnest* of our inheritance unto the redemption of God's own possession, unto the praise of his glory . . . Grieve not the Holy Spirit of God, in whom ye were *sealed* unto the day of redemption" (Eph. 1:13-14; 4:30).

"Now he that stablisheth us with you in Christ, and anointed us, is God; who also *sealed* us and gave us the *earnest* of the Spirit in our hearts" (II Cor. 1:21-22). God hereby declares that we belong to Him forever and that the Spirit within us is the first installment and guarantee of that full redemption which we shall receive in glory. And it is the Spirit who keeps us faithful in view of eternal salvation; without His presence and support we should be powerless to persevere unto the end. Wherefore Paul wrote to Timothy, "That good thing which was committed unto thee guard through the Holy Spirit which dwelleth in us" (II Tim. 1:14).

What joy to be able to build one's life upon such certainty and to rejoice in the possession of God's salvation!

CHAPTER 6

THE SPIRIT'S DWELLING IN THE HEART OF THE BELIEVER

I. THE IMPORTANCE AND CERTAINTY OF THIS FACT

THE SPIRIT OF GOD does not only regenerate, baptize, adopt and seal the believer; having done all this He does not abandon him and return to Heaven; He makes His dwelling in the believer.

It has already been remarked that one of the basic characteristics of this present dispensation is that God places His Spirit *within us*. For this reason Jesus said to His disciples during the days of His humiliation: "It is expedient for you that I go away, for if I go not away the Comforter will not come unto you; but if I go I will send him unto you. . . . And I will pray the Father and he shall give you another Comforter that he may be with you forever, even the Spirit of truth; . . . ye know him, for he abideth with you and shall be in you" (John 16:7; 14:16-17). The spiritual presence of God the Saviour in the hearts of all believers is the indispensable complement of the work of Jesus Christ. During His life on earth, His presence could only be bestowed temporarily and externally to a small group of men in a given country. Now Christ dwells, through the Spirit, in the hearts of all those who love Him within the compass of the whole world.

This wonderful statement is repeated in a great number of passages in the Gospels and the epistles. Jesus, on another occasion announced in these terms that He would live in the hearts of His disciples: "He that eateth my flesh and drinketh my blood, abideth in me and *I in him*. . . . In that day ye shall know that I am in the Father, and ye in me, and *I in you*. . . . Abide in me and *I in you*. . . . I made known unto them thy name. . . . that the love wherewith thou lovedst me may be in them, and *I in them*" (John 6:56; 14:20; 15:4; 17:26). Paul, writing to the Romans, says: "But ye are not in the flesh but in the Spirit, if so be that *the Spirit of God dwelleth in you*. But if any man have not the Spirit of Christ he is none of his. And if *Christ is in you*, the body is dead because of sin, but the Spirit is life because of righteousness. But if the Spirit of him that raised up Jesus from the dead *dwelleth in you*, he that raised up Christ Jesus from the dead shall quicken also your mortal bodies through *his Spirit that dwelleth in you*" (Rom. 8:9-11). Three times in this passage does the Apostle use the conditional: "If the Spirit of God dwelleth in you . . ." which implies "if you are true believers the Spirit dwelleth in you," since he adds that without this abiding presence none can belong to Christ (v. 9).

This truth, so important and yet so simple, is scarcely perceived by our spirit which experiences difficulty in grasping such a gift by faith alone. In the present day many of God's children are unaware that the Spirit of God dwells in them, and even the apostle Paul, asked the Corinthians on three occasions this vital question: "*Know ye not* that ye are a temple of God and that the Spirit of God dwelleth in you? If any man destroyeth the temple of God, him shall God destroy; for the temple of God is holy, which temple ye are. . . . Or, *know ye not* that your body is a temple of the Holy Ghost which is in you, which ye have from God? and ye are not your own. Or, *know ye not* as to your own selves that Jesus Christ is in you? Unless indeed ye be reprobate" (I Cor. 3:16-17; 6:19; II Cor. 13:5).

If present-day believers, who possess the whole New Testament for their enlightenment, fail to recognize this precious truth, they are greatly to blame and deprive themselves of an inexhaustible source of joy and power. For what could we achieve without the constant help and presence of the Comforter?

Paul, writing still to the Corinthians, says, "We are a temple of the living God, even as God hath said" (II Cor. 6:16). And then to Timothy he writes: "That good thing which was committed unto thee guard through the Holy Ghost which dwelleth in us" (II Tim. 1:14).

In his first epistle, John is just as definite: "And as for you the anointing [i.e., the Holy Spirit] which ye received of him, *abideth in you* and ye need not that anyone teach you; but as his anointing teacheth you concerning all things, and is true and is no lie and even as it taught you, abide ye in him. . . . Whosoever is begotten of God doeth no sin, because his seed *abideth in him* [this seed is that new nature, the Holy Spirit within the believer]. . . . And he that keepeth his commandments abideth in him and *he in him.* And hereby we know that *he abideth in us* by the Spirit which he gave us. . . . Greater is *he that is in you* than he that is in the world. . . . If we love one another God *abideth in us* and his love is perfected in us; and hereby know we that we *abide in him,* and he in us because he hath given us of his Spirit. . . . Whosoever shall confess that Jesus is the Son of God, God *abideth in him* and he in God" (I John 2:27; 3:9, 24; 4:4, 12-13, 15).

Lastly James adds: "That Spirit which he made to *dwell in us* yearneth for us even unto jealous envy" (James 4:5, R.V. marg.). Here then is a certain fact abundantly illustrated: God gives the Holy Spirit that He may dwell in the heart of every believer.

II. Does the Spirit Alone Dwell in Us?

This is an important question. Some might think that, in truth, having once received the Spirit who is the third Person of the Trinity, they had, in a sense, no further need of the other two Persons. The Holy Spirit would replace, and put to one side, if one dare to say so, the Father and the Son. It is, in fact, not so, as Scripture clearly shows:

1. Together with the Spirit, God the Father, reveals His presence within us.

To prove this we have but to recall to mind all those texts drawn from the First Epistle of John, quoted above. Of these we shall but mention again the following: "He that keepeth his commandments abideth in him and he [i.e., God] in him. And hereby know we that he abideth in us, by the Spirit which he gave us" (I John 3:24). Paul remarks that each believer is "a temple of God" and that the congregation of believers, forming the Church, is "builded together for a habitation of God in the Spirit" (I Cor. 3:16; Eph. 2:22).

2. With the Spirit we receive also the presence of God the Son.

Paul's prayer for the Ephesians was that they might be "strengthened with power through his Spirit in the inner man, that Christ may dwell in your hearts through faith" (Eph. 3: 16-17).

Moreover this same apostle, when speaking of the divine presence in our hearts, mentions interchangeably God, Christ or the Holy Spirit. He exclaims: "I live, and yet no longer I but Christ liveth in me" (Gal. 2:20). He summarizes spiritual life in the following words: "Christ in you, the hope of glory" (Col. 1:27). Lastly, Christ Himself declared that "If a man love me, he will keep my words, and my Father will love him and we [i.e., the Father and the Son] will come unto him and make our abode with him" (John 14:23).

Thus with the Spirit comes the whole glorious Trinity to dwell in us. What an inconceivable honor! Words fail to express our wonder and gratitude before the greatness of God's salvation.

Nevertheless, if we pause to consider, we should not be surprised at the fact that the Spirit does not come alone to dwell in us. The three Persons of the Trinity are one and do not act independently. At one time they may have appeared to be dissociated, during the Son's earthly life; and yet, the Father and the Spirit were within Him accompanying Him ceaselessly. Since His glorification they have fully reassumed their eternal relationship and now these three Persons dwell in us, pursuing together their work of perfect redemption.

III. How Long Does the Spirit Dwell Within Us?

Many Christians are prepared to believe that the Spirit was given them and came to dwell in their hearts at the time of conversion; but they also believe that after certain falls the Spirit withdrew and abandoned them. Is this the teaching of Scripture? On the contrary, Jesus said to His disciples: "I will pray the Father and he shall give you another Comforter that he may be with you *forever,* even the Spirit of truth" (John 14:16). Thus the Spirit is given us not for a limited time, but forever. Were He to leave us, for one moment only, we should instantly lose spiritual life and relapse into death, for our life is Christ and He remains within us only through the Spirit. Under the Old Covenant the Spirit would be withdrawn, but that is no longer the case now. Cannot a sincere believer lose the Spirit? We believe not and think, to the contrary, that he will prove the sincerity of his faith and the truth of his regeneration in persevering to the end, submitting himself to God's chastisement for reconciliation and sanctification. (In this connection refer to the remarks on the sin against the Holy Spirit and Christians [see page 64].)

We must beware, however, of living according to the flesh and refusing to be sanctified progressively, under the pretext that the Spirit dwells in us eternally. What happens then, when a child of God has sinned and not yet confessed and abandoned his sin? The Spirit is grieved and immediately ceases to manifest His power. This will be dealt with in the following chapter.

IV. When, and in Whom Does the Spirit Make His Abode?

1. The Spirit dwells in the hearts of God's children from the moment when they believe in the Saviour.

Jesus, speaking to His disciples, told them that the Father would send them the Spirit of truth "whom the world [i.e., the unconverted] cannot receive; for it beholdeth him not, neither knoweth him; ye know him, for he abideth with you and shall be in you" (John 14:17). It is obvious that those who reject Jesus Christ shall not receive the Spirit. On the other hand the only condition necessary for the indwelling of the Spirit is the heart's acceptance of the Saviour through faith: "Whosoever shall confess that Jesus is the Son of God, God abideth in him, and he in God" (I John 4:15). "Behold, I stand at the door and knock; if any man hear my voice and open the door, I will come in to him and will sup with him and he with me" (Rev. 3:20). "If a man love me [herein lies the great condition], he will keep my word, and my Father will love him, and we will come unto him and make our abode with him" (John 14:23). Paul expresses the same thought when he prays for the Ephesians, that Christ might dwell in their hearts *through faith* (Eph. 3:17).

Obviously this faith in the Saviour must be sincere and followed by works made possible by the Spirit's presence within us. This is the meaning of the following passages: "He that keepeth his commandments abideth in him and he in him. . . . If we love one another, God abideth in us" (I John 3:24; 4:12). For faith without works is dead and the Spirit of God will not dwell in the heart of one who wishes to remain in death. Nevertheless, the Spirit does not take up His abode in us after we have been sanctified (as many believers think). On the contrary He comes to us *in order* to sanctify us, at that very moment when, coming to Christ as we are, we accept Him through faith as the Saviour.

2. Does the Spirit, therefore, dwell in the hearts of all regenerated believers?

Some think that the constant presence of the Spirit is granted only to the most mature of God's children after undergoing certain experiences following upon regeneration. On the contrary, however, it is quite definite that the Spirit dwells in the hearts of *all* regenerated believers, without exception. For, indeed without His presence, no man belongs to Christ. "If any man have not the Spirit of Christ he is none of his." The same passage adds, "For as many as are led by the Spirit of God, these are sons of God" (Rom. 8:9, 14). Paul further says, "Because ye are sons, God sent forth the Spirit of his Son into our hearts crying Abba, Father" (Gal. 4:6). Then with regard to the new man with which every believer must be clothed, he writes: "There cannot be Greek and Jew, circumcision and uncircumcision, barbarian, Scythian, bondman, freeman: but Christ is all and *in all*" (Col. 3:11). God, therefore, sends the Spirit to dwell in the hearts of *all* His children.

Jesus, Himself, moreover, included all believers without any exception when He declared: "The Spirit of truth . . . abideth with you and shall be in you . . . If any man love me . . . we will make our abode with him" (John 14:17, 23).

Lastly, the Parable of the Ten Virgins also teaches us that the characteristic mark of the true believer is that he has oil in his lamp, that is to say, the Holy Spirit in his heart (Matt. 25:1, 12). Without this presence he cannot be saved.

V. CAN A BELIEVER KNOW WHETHER THE SPIRIT IS DWELLING WITHIN HIM?

Yes, indeed, for Jesus' words are quite positive: "The Father . . . shall give you . . . the Spirit of truth: whom the world cannot receive; for it beholdeth him not, neither knoweth him; *ye know him*, for he abideth with you and shall be in you. . . . In that day *ye shall know that I am* in my Father, and ye in me, and *I in you*" (John 14:17, 20).

Many of God's children, however, are not conscious of the presence of the Spirit, for various reasons:

1. Certain Christians are often entirely ignorant of this great truth and unaware of those clear and numerous Biblical texts which reveal it to us. For Jesus said, "Ye shall know the truth, and the truth shall make you free" (John 8:32). It is obvious that on account of their neglect of reading and meditating upon the Word of God, coupled with ignorance of their most precious privileges, such Christians cannot be freed nor can they progress spiritually.

2. Others know that the Spirit must dwell in their hearts, but they seek to base the certainty of His presence on their feelings. If they feel happy, at peace, and strong they think that the Spirit is in them; if, on the other hand, their hearts are void and sad, they are persuaded that the Spirit has never dwelt in them, or that He has departed from them. For our spiritual life there cannot be a more unstable basis than that of feelings. Relying on them is tantamount to walking by sight and not by faith; it is, in fact, unbelief. Jesus' words to us are: "Said I not unto thee that if thou believest, thou shouldest see the glory of God?" We seek to do the opposite, to see and feel first.

May we, therefore, learn to believe that the Spirit is in us, children of God, simply because the Bible tells us so. Then, when we have believed (and not before) we shall see this Spirit bring forth in our hearts that love, joy and peace which we had hitherto sought in vain (Gal. 5:22, 23).

3. In the majority of cases, alas, believers remain unconscious of the Spirit's presence because unconfessed sins interrupt their communion with God. The Spirit is nevertheless in them, but He is grieved and His power is hindered from being clearly revealed. If this be the case with us, let us hasten to confess our faults to God, seeking cleansing in His purifying blood. Then immediately we shall receive that joy consequent upon His presence.

CONCLUSION

At the close of this chapter let us ask ourselves whether the Spirit of God does, indeed, dwell in us. If the answer be *Yes*, how can we remain weak and discouraged? The divine presence within us is that very source of living water which fully quenches our thirst, springing up, inexhaustibly, unto eternal life (John 4:14). There is no need for us to seek for strength and support elsewhere; Christ is in us, the hope of glory (Col. 1:27). But we must remind ourselves that for this very reason we must glorify God in our bodies and our spirits which have become His temple. If, on the other hand, we do not yet know this divine Guest, why do we not receive Him this very day? Christ stands knocking at our door desiring to enter within us forever. Let us open the door to Him, and His Spirit, taking possession of our whole being, will cause rivers of living water to flow through us.

CHAPTER 7

GRIEVE NOT THE HOLY SPIRIT

WE HAVE JUST SEEN that all true believers have received the Holy Spirit who dwells within them. How then can we explain the inconsistencies and lack of power prevalent among so many of them? The reason is that they have failed to obey the commandment found in Ephesians 4:30: "Grieve not the Holy Spirit of God, in whom ye were sealed unto the day of redemption."

I. IT IS POSSIBLE TO GRIEVE THE SPIRIT

The way in which God respects man's liberty is truly extraordinary. Even as He forces no unbeliever to be converted, so He never compels a believer to become sanctified. In bestowing upon us His Spirit of holiness, the Saviour might well have imposed His will upon us in all things, forcing us in that very instant to abandon sin in all its forms. His aim is, indeed, to free us from evil by a close responsiveness to His will; but His desire is that we should consent to do this of our own free will. He leaves with us the formidable possibility of resisting His sublime presence and of grieving His Holy Spirit who is within us. What a responsibility is ours if we fail to respond to such goodness!

Let us note again that the expression "grieving the Spirit" is characteristic. Not only does it imply the personification of the Spirit but also that He is infinitely sensitive and that He loves us. If it were otherwise we should be able only to resist Him, and not to cause Him sorrow on our behalf.

106

II. HOW CAN WE GRIEVE THE SPIRIT?

Let the Bible answer this question.

1. The verse which bids us not grieve the Spirit (Eph. 4:30) is framed by exhortations which throw added light upon this commandment (Eph. 4:25; 5:18). Here Paul lists various sins which we must avoid on pain of wounding the Spirit. Naturally this list is not complete; other things there are which grieve the Spirit and which are not mentioned here. But let us limit ourselves to giving our attention to those practical examples which it affords us. Among others, the following sins grieve the Spirit:

> Lying (Eph. 4:25)
> Anger (v. 26).
> Theft (v. 28).

Evil speaking—speech that is dishonest, impure, foolish, unseemly, jesting (v. 29; 5:3, 4). Evil feelings (bitterness, wrath, spite), clamor, railing (v. 31). The absence of goodness, forgiveness and love (v. 32; 5:2). Fornication, uncleanness, covetousness, greed (5:3). All that is evil and which has to be committed in secret and under cover of darkness (vv. 11, 12). Drunkenness, etc. (v. 18).

2. The names given to the Holy Spirit also teach us how we may grieve Him.

He is the Spirit of *holiness* (Rom. 1:4). All impurity, all filthiness, any contact with evil grieves Him.

He is the Spirit of *wisdom, understanding* and *knowledge* (Isa. 11:2). When we remain in ignorance of spiritual truths, lack zeal in the reading and study of the Bible, and prefer the obscure teachings of men to His, we grieve Him.

He is the Spirit of *life* and of *power* (Rom. 8:2; II Tim. 1:7). Spiritual death, or weakness, arrested development, and lack of power in our testimony—all these grieve Him.

He is the Spirit of *truth* (John 14:17). All lying, all intended falsehood, heresy, all false appearances and attitudes, all hypocrisy, grieve Him.

He is the Spirit of *faith* (II Cor. 4:13). Our doubts, discouragement, anxieties and constant querying, grieve Him.

He is the Spirit of *love* and of *grace* (II Tim. 1:7; Heb. 10:29). If there is in us hardness of heart, any refusal of forgiveness, any bitterness, any complaining; or if our hearts remain obdurate when faced with the suffering and perdition of souls, if we are lukewarm toward God, the Spirit is grieved.

Finally let us point out that He is the Spirit of *glory* (I Peter 4:14). That which is of the flesh, mundane and earthly in our hearts, grieves Him.

If possible, study in the same manner the other names accorded to the Spirit as detailed on page 12.

These few texts show us with what ease we can grieve the Spirit; many more could be quoted, but the lesson for us would still be the same; every sin consciously committed, whatever its nature, whether great or small, open or hidden, grieves the Spirit.

May we who read these lines pause a moment to examine our own consciences. Is there not, at this very instant, in our hearts one of those things mentioned above, fettering our spiritual life and debarring us from full communion with God? If, standing before the mirror of the Word, we are conscious of having grieved the Spirit, may we bow before God in humiliation and repentance that He may pardon and purify us.

III. WHAT ARE THE CONSEQUENCES OF GRIEVING THE SPIRIT?

1. Does the Spirit depart from us when grieved?

That is what many Christians do believe. But it has already been noted that it was under the Old Covenant that the Spirit could be withdrawn (see page 30). From Pentecost up to the present time He has been granted, to dwell within us forevermore (John 14:16). Therefore He does not depart from us if we commit some fault, but convicts us of sin.

2. If we grieve the Spirit, we forego both power and joy as well as communion with God.

God respects our liberty; as soon as we elect to sin rather than obey His will, He suspends His activity within our hearts and breaks His communion with us. From then onward the power of the Spirit is no longer made manifest through us; we stand powerless before the Tempter and suffer one defeat after another. Realizing such a weakness in their spiritual life and witness, many cry out to God praying at length while despairingly fighting for victory, for they imagine that the Saviour has no wish to help or is withholding His assistance for a while. But the truth is that the obstacle lies in themselves. So long as the Spirit is grieved He will take no step toward their deliverance.

The Old Testament, particularly the Books of Joshua and Judges, holds much instruction on this point. For example, on account of Achan's secret sin, the Lord ceased to manifest Himself to Israel and forebore to bring them victory. He declared to Joshua: "I will not be with you any more except ye destroy the devoted thing among you. . . . There is a devoted thing in the midst of thee, O Israel; thou canst not stand before thine enemies until ye take away the devoted thing from among you" (Josh. 7:12, 13). The Tabernacle, in the which God had placed His presence, was still among the people but that presence had ceased to act for them.

In similar fashion, today, the Spirit, though grieved, still dwells in the temple of our body but no longer reveals Himself. Our prayers seem to reach no further than the ceiling, and our hearts remain arid and cheerless. If we grieve the Spirit not only do we lose power and communion but also joy; and the fruit of the Spirit is joy (see Gal. 5:22). Once sin has crept into us, the Spirit ceases to impart His joy to us. Is it not a common experience that once we have committed a fault, sorrow overwhelms us and engulfs our hearts? It is the sorrow of the Spirit Himself. Herein lies the reason why so many

Christians lack both joy and attraction. May we eliminate the causes of this sorrow and thus taste and spread abroad that perfect joy which is so freely given us in Jesus Christ.

3. What will happen if we willfully persist in grieving the Spirit?

As we have seen, the Bible definitely states that the Spirit dwells eternally in our hearts. Nevertheless it solemnly warns us against adopting that line of argument which can be summed up thus: Since the Spirit remains forever within me I can indulge in sin without fear that He shall leave me," or as Paul expressed it: "Shall we continue in sin that grace may abound?" (Rom. 6:1). Let us not delude ourselves; we cannot trifle with God. "The Spirit which he made to dwell in us he yearneth for even unto jealous envy" (James 4:5, R.V. marg.)

In Isaiah 63:10 we find these formidable words: "But they rebelled and grieved his Holy Spirit; therefore he was turned to be their enemy and himself fought against them." The situation is the same for us if we deliberately provoke the Spirit by sin and do not seek to become sanctified through Him. Other passages state quite distinctly that "if ye live after the flesh, ye must die" (Rom. 8:13). "A man that hath set at nought Moses's law dieth without compassion on the word of two or three witnesses; of how much sorer punishment, think ye, shall he be judged worthy, who hath trodden under foot the Son of God and hath counted the blood of the covenant, wherewith he was sanctified, an unholy thing and hath done despite unto the Spirit of grace?" (Heb. 10:28, 29). Despite to the Spirit of grace consists not of sinning and consequently grieving Him, whether once or on many occasions; for what believer is there, who though growing in spiritual stature, has not been made conscious of sins recently committed or until then unknown? In this passage despite to the Spirit means willful sin by maintaining before Him an attitude of open revolt and by rejecting utterly the Son of God and the blood of the covenant. Scripture informs that it is possible to stand in opposition to the

Spirit, as the Israelites constantly did (Acts 7:51), and urges us not to "quench the Spirit" (I Thess. 5:19).

All these expressions show us that there can be a terrible progression in man's resistance toward God. Would a real child of God come to such a pass? It is unlikely, as has already been suggested. By persevering to the end he will show that eternal life has indeed taken root in him. On the other hand, one who falls into such an abyss will give proof that his heart lacks sincerity and has never belonged in truth to Christ. Indeed Jesus Himself shall say to those who have prophesied and done miracles in His name, but have nevertheless stayed without, "I never knew you; depart from me ye that work iniquity" (Matt. 7:22-23). May these exhortations reveal to us the dangers that lie in grieving the Spirit, and may they teach us to do so no longer.

IV. WHEN THE SPIRIT HAS BEEN GRIEVED WHAT MUST BE DONE?

Frequently, thinking that the Spirit has abandoned them, or even that they have committed the unpardonable sin, believers give themselves up to despair. Yet, if they are burdened with their fault and regret it they can have the perfect assurance of finding pardon provided they follow the instructions contained in Scripture.

1. We must first confess our sins.

"If we confess our sins, he is faithful and righteous to forgive us our sins and to cleanse us from all unrighteousness" (I John 1:9). Nothing can take the place of confession. We may weep, pray, work for God, or make great financial sacrifices, but none of these will restore to us the peace that comes from on high. God desires that we ask pardon of Him for our failings, for so long as they remain unconfessed, our pride remains unbroken: "He that covereth his transgressions shall not prosper, but whoso confesseth and forsaketh them shall obtain mercy" (Prov. 28:13). In confession it is not enough to say

"Lord, forgive me if I have sinned." We must lay before God, naming them individually, all those sins of which the Holy Spirit has made us conscious.

When must such a confession be made? As soon as we feel within us the sorrow of the Holy Spirit and become aware of our fault. Sins usually do not come singly. If we delay, if we wish to wait, before setting things aright, until the evening or the following Sunday or the coming meeting, we are in grave danger; other sins will creep into us, our soul will lose its motive force and we shall be in danger of retrogressing. For this reason, wherever we may be, we should make *immediate* confession of our sin; at home, in the street, at work or while traveling, let us cry out to God and He will forgive us. There will have been a break in our communion with Him but it will not have had time to grow worse and without great delay we shall be able to resume our forward progress. Naturally, confession must first be made to God who alone can pardon. But if we have offended our neighbor we must ask forgiveness of him too. "If therefore thou art offering thy gift at the altar and there rememberest that thy brother hath ought against thee, leave thy gift before the altar and go thy way, first be reconciled to thy brother and then come and offer thy gift" (Matt. 5:23-24). James 5:16 adds, "Confess therefore, your sins one to another," which means "ask for mutual forgiveness if you have sinned one against another." By reason of their unwillingness to do this many have failed to regain communion with God, even though they may have confessed to Him in private all their shortcomings.

2. We must then believe in God's pardon.

It is not enough merely to confess our faults to God or to men. We must grasp pardon through faith. Such faith should not consist of a vague hope in God's patience and goodness; it must have as its definite foundation the person and expiatory work of the Saviour. John makes it very clear for us. After first saying "If we confess our sins, he is faithful and righteous to forgive us our sins and to cleanse us from all unrighteousness," he goes on immediately to explain this process of purification: "Jesus Christ . . . is the propitiation for our sins"; "the blood of Jesus, his Son, cleanseth us from all sin" (I John 1: 7, 9; 2:2). If a man comes to God and confesses his sins and does not at the same time seek the protection of the blood of the cross, he will not be purified but condemned.

We have an example of this in the numberless Israelites who confessed their sins in accepting the baptism of John the Baptist. This confession should have prepared them to accept Jesus Christ, but for many of them it was of no value because they believed neither on the Messiah when He was revealed to them, nor in His works. Let us be quite clear on these two points: if we have sinned, have we already confessed our failure? And having confessed, do we believe that we are fully purified by the blood of Jesus? Note further that if we do these two things God cleanses our hearts from *all unrighteousness* (I John 1: 9). In consequence, from that moment, the Spirit, no longer grieved, can once again reveal His power and life within us.

3. Lastly, what must we do in order to avoid grieving the Spirit again?

A sincere believer will not remain content with the knowledge of how he may regain pardon and peace after sinning. He will long from the depth of his heart to gain victory over evil and no longer grieve the Spirit. How shall he attain this? If hitherto he has so easily fallen into sin, being powerless before temptation, it is because he lacked an indispensable experience: he was not filled with the Spirit. We shall now turn our attention to the Bible's teaching on this question.

CHAPTER 8

THE FULLNESS OF THE HOLY SPIRIT

LET US FIRST DEFINE what we mean by "the fullness of the Holy Spirit." The Bible does not contain this expression as it stands, but in a number of passages it speaks of the possibility and the necessity for the believer to be "filled with the Holy Spirit." If, therefore, we sometimes speak of the "fullness of the Holy Spirit" we do so for convenience' sake and imply by it the "fact of being filled with the Spirit."

I. THE SPIRIT'S FILLING INDISPENSABLE TO ALL BELIEVERS

Up till this point we have come to see that the soul is first convicted of sin, then regenerated, baptized, sealed and inhabited by the Spirit. All these operations on the part of the Spirit are yet not enough to bring about sanctification, for the soul must still be filled with the Spirit. This assertion is demonstrated in the two following cases which have already been quoted above. The Corinthians were all baptized of the Holy Spirit and had received the Spirit whose temple they were. But they remained carnal Christians, babes in Christ unable to bear anything stronger than milk (I Cor. 12:13; 6:19; 3:1-3). The Galatians also had all been baptized in Christ; they had put on Christ and God had placed His Spirit in their hearts. Despite this they were turning away from the true Gospel, seeking perfection in the flesh and causing Paul to fear that he had worked in vain on their behalf (Gal. 3:27; 4:6; 1:6; 3:3; 4:11). The Spirit is thus unable to accomplish fully His work in a heart which is not filled by Him.

II. JESUS, HIMSELF SPOKE IN ADVANCE OF THAT FULLNESS WHICH THE SPIRIT WOULD BRING TO BELIEVERS

Calling Himself the Good Shepherd, He said: "I came that they [i.e., His sheep] may have life and may have it abundantly" (John 10:10). Yet, how many of God's children have already received life by new birth but are sick or spiritually weak because they never experience this abundance! To this Samaritan woman Jesus declared: "Whosoever drinketh of the water that I shall give him shall never thirst; but the water that I shall give him shall become in him a well of water springing up into eternal life" (John 4:14). To the Jews He added, "I am the bread of life; he that cometh unto me shall not hunger and he that believeth on me shall never thirst. . . . If any man thirst, let him come unto me and drink. He that believeth, as the Scripture hath said, out of his belly shall flow rivers of living water" (John 6:35; 7:37-38).

Can we say of our own selves that we no longer hunger and thirst and that rivers of living waters flow from us? Yet Jesus Christ's promise is quite explicit, and how greatly we need to act upon it! How is this abundance of life, promised by the Saviour, imparted to us? John 7:39 tells us quite clearly: "This spake he of the Spirit which they that believed on him were to receive." It is, in fact, the divine presence which becomes in us that eternal source of living water fully supplying all our needs provided that we are filled with the Spirit.

But, some will say, is it really possible to be filled by the Spirit? Have others before us really experienced this?

III. THE FIRST DISCIPLES WERE ALL FILLED WITH THE SPIRIT

The Book of Acts teaches us that being filled with the Spirit was a normal experience in the Early Church.

1. The apostles and the leaders of the Church were filled with the Spirit.

Peter when speaking with confidence before the priests and elders of Israel on the occasion of his first arrest, was filled with the Spirit as was also Barnabas at Antioch (Acts 4:8; 11:24). Similarly with Paul when he silenced Elymas the sorcerer (Acts 13:9).

When it came to nominating the deacons to deal with material concerns, it was required that they should be not only converted but also full of the Holy Spirit and of wisdom (Acts 6:3). (Would that in the present day, these same conditions were imposed on all servants of God! What a transformation would result in our religious circles!)

Finally Stephen remained steadfast in the face of hatred and even death, because he was filled with the Holy Spirit (Acts 7:55).

2. The assembly of the disciples underwent the same experience.

It might have been asked whether the fullness of the Spirit was reserved only for the great men of God called to some special task. But from the Acts we learn that it was the ordinary experience of all believers; the one hundred and twenty, on the day of Pentecost, were *all* filled with the Spirit (Acts 2:4). Yet these hundred and twenty people were, in great part, simple disciples whose names even are unknown to us. After Pentecost the Church increased rapidly and its numbers were swollen to *five thousand*. This crowd gathered to welcome back Peter and John after their first arrest and we are told that "when they had prayed the place was shaken wherein they were gathered together, and they were all filled with the Holy Ghost and they spoke the Word of God with boldness" (Acts 4:4, 31).

If the assembly of the believers of that epoch were filled with the Spirit, how is it that this truth is so unknown in our day? Besides, if, in the Early Church, *all* the disciples had this experience, can you not also have it even if you are the most humble and the least known among believers?

3. Even the newly converted were filled with the Holy Spirit. To Saul of Tarsus, three days after his meeting with the risen Christ, Ananias declared, "The Lord, even Jesus . . . hath sent me that thou mayest receive thy sight and be filled with the Holy Ghost" (Acts 9:17). Here again it might be objected that Saul was a special case. But Acts 13:52 tells us of the disciples at Antioch in Pisidia to whom Paul preached for a few weeks at the most. At the time of his departure he leaves them filled with joy and with the Holy Spirit.

Let us not think of the fullness of the Spirit as an experience of necessity both rare and unattainable. As God, in the Early Church, gave it to each, even so does He desire that all of us should possess it today.

IV. GOD COMMANDS ALL BELIEVERS IN ALL AGES TO BE FILLED WITH THE HOLY SPIRIT

Through the medium of Paul's letters He commands us to be "not drunken with wine wherein is riot, but . . . filled with the Spirit" (Eph. 5:18). It is clear that these instructions cover all epochs and include all of God's children. Doubtless we seek to obey the first of these commandments for we know that drunkards shall not inherit the kingdom of God. But have we understood that the second commandment, to be filled with the Spirit, applies to us also, and have we striven to comply with it? If we have not, we need seek no further explanation for our defeats and spiritual weakness.

It is, nevertheless, easy to understand that God wishes to fill us with His Spirit. He knows that we cannot serve two masters. Moreover from the moment when He makes His abode in us, His desire is that His Spirit may completely overwhelm us to sanctify and to free us, transforming us into His image. Does not any father desire the fullness of health and strength for his child? God can only give us this fullness when we allow ourselves to be dominated by the Spirit. Then again, Scripture tells us that God yearneth, even unto jealous envy, for the

Spirit whom He has made to dwell in us (James 4:5, R. V. marg.). How then could He fail to desire that this Spirit alone should reign in our hearts?

If we, therefore, wish to please God and know the truly Christian life, let us obey His explicit command. Failure to seek the fullness of the Spirit is tantamount to resisting His most holy will toward His children.

V. WHAT IS THE MEANING AND THE IMPLICATION OF BEING FILLED WITH THE SPIRIT?

From the start let us observe what has been frequently pointed out that the fullness of the Spirit does not imply that *we* have more of the Spirit at our disposal, but, to the contrary that He possesses more of us and holds us entirely at His disposal.

The Spirit in us is like an overwhelming force; He immediately occupies every particle of our being that we relinquish to Him, even as the air immediately fills any empty space to which it is given access. That is why we have nothing extraordinary to do to be filled with the Spirit. From the moment that we abandon ourselves in all sincerity to God, as we stand and to the best of our ability, believing in His promise, we are filled by His Spirit to the measure of our capacity. Thus all men, even a new convert lacking experience and greater knowledge can undergo this wonderful experience.

In this connection Jesus Christ Himself used the following image: He compared the Spirit to a well which, springing up in our hearts, fills them completely until they finally overflow with an abundance of living water (John 4:14; 7:38-39). The water of this inexhaustible well overruns, of its own accord—we might almost say automatically—the small space which surrounds it, washing from it all impurities, but on one condition only: namely that its passage should not be blocked by the rock of our rebellious will. The Spirit in us will carry away all obstacles and overcome all resistance, but never will

He so act unless He has the support of our own will which He respects. If this will opposes Him, He will be grieved and will no longer manifest Himself; if, however, it abandons itself to entire submission to Him, He will fill us on the instant.

Let us not forget that the Spirit within us is the presence of Christ. If we are filled with the Spirit, it is Christ Himself who fills us. For we know that "in him dwelleth all the fullness of the Godhead bodily" and that "in Him ye are made full" (Col. 2:9-10). Christ is the source of life, victory and purity, of love and sanctification, in short, of fullness; and this source is within me. If it fills me, in accordance with God's will, all these gifts will be given me. Though to many Christians it seems unattainable, I can say through faith that from the time of my new birth "yet no longer I but Christ liveth in me" (Gal. 2:20). And if I am filled with Christ His life will increasingly reveal itself in me and through me.

Oh, how great is the depth of the riches, the wisdom and the knowledge of God! Lord, reveal to me by Thy Spirit of Truth how I may attain such blessing.

VI. WHAT MUST WE DO TO BECOME FILLED WITH THE SPIRIT?

It would appear that the Scripture mentions four essential conditions.

1. We must confess to God all the sins of which we are conscious and allow ourselves to be purified by the blood of the cross. In the preceding chapter we noted that the smallest sin grieves the Holy Spirit, and forthwith prevents Him from revealing Himself. The Spirit will fill us only if He is no longer grieved and our hearts are purified from all iniquity by faith in the blood of Christ (I John 1:9). Let us examine our consciences and let nothing remain which separates us from God. In particular may we confess that, by our own failure, we are not filled with the Spirit and may we be humbled by our disobedience.

2. We must desire and seek for the fullness of the Spirit.

Jesus said, "If any man thirst let him come unto me and drink. . . . He that believeth on me . . . out of his belly shall flow rivers of living water. . . . This spake he of the Spirit which they that believed on him were to receive" (John 7:37-39).

Many self-styled Christians have no spiritual thirst. They are satisfied with themselves, their faith, piety and good works. They lean for support on past experiences and think it sufficient to have professed conversion some years before. They forget that new birth (if they have experienced it) is but the first step in the Christian life and that they must grow "unto the measure of the stature of the fullness of Christ" (Eph. 4:13) as they "follow after . . . sanctification without which no man shall see the Lord" (Heb. 12:14). What the Lord wrote to the church of Laodicea might be said of them also, "Thou sayest, I am rich and have gotten riches and have need of nothing; and knowest not that thou art the wretched one and miserable and poor and blind and naked" (Rev. 3:17). There is no hope for those who have no spiritual needs.

But on the other hand, thirst is an imperative need which must be satisfied. A man racked by thirst will give anything to be able to quench it. Fullness, life through the Spirit, is given only to those who truly thirst, to those who are prepared to pay the price, to abandon all if necessary to receive it. "Blessed are they that hunger and thirst after righteousness, for they shall be filled" (Matt. 5:6). Have we such a thirst for sanctification, victory and plenty, for radiance and power? Do we desire a Christian life which is free from constant vicissitudes and repeated falls, unencumbered by weakness and continual sorrow? In short do we thirst after the Spirit's fullness? Then let us draw near to the Saviour for His promise is to us.

3. We must unreservedly yield ourselves to God, giving access in our whole being to His influence.

We have seen that God wishes to fill us with His Spirit. But only what is empty can be filled. Undoubtedly, if we are converted, the Spirit has occupied a certain amount of room in us, but is every part of our being open to admit Him? Or have we perhaps brought to God only those sins which inconvenience us, for which we cared not overmuch, while retaining several idols and, above all, our own wills? It is self-evident that our refusal to yield every sphere of our life, be it only in one thing, hinders the Lord from filling us. He wants us a hundred per cent for Him and gives us the choice — all or nothing; take it or leave it. Jesus says to us, "Whosoever he be of you that renounceth not all that he hath, he cannot be my disciple. . . . For whosoever would save his life shall lose it, but whosoever shall lose his life [What more can we surrender?] for my sake, the same shall save it" (Luke 14:33; 9:24). We can choose to be lukewarm, to refuse knowledge of sanctification as the fullness of life, but the Lord will say to us, "Because thou art . . . neither hot nor cold, I will spue thee out of my mouth" (Rev. 3:16).

Some, perhaps, will say: I would willingly yield all into God's hands and empty my heart that He might fill it, but there are many things which keep me bound and which I am unable to root out of my life. But, of course, God does not expect us to purify ourselves or to expel first by our own efforts, that which hinders His work in us. We would not accomplish this. All He asks of us is our consent to let Him enter into every part that He may transform and purify all. All He desires is the complete submission of our will contrary to which He will not act, since He created us free beings. But once full command has been placed in His hands, He will no longer be hindered from filling us and glorifying Himself in us. According to His promise He will produce in us both the will and the ability to act (Phil. 2:13), and will make all things possible. Listen to the exhortation of the apostle Paul, who gives us the key to sanctification: "Present yourselves unto God as alive from the dead. . . . I beseech you therefore . . . present your bodies, a living sacrifice, holy, acceptable to God, which is your reasonable service" (Rom. 6:13; 12:1).

May we present ourselves unto God saying to Him, "Lord, I yield myself completely to Thee as I am; I am willing to pay the price, cost what it may, and to be filled with Thy Spirit."

4. Lastly, we must believe that God has filled us with His Spirit once we have carried out the first three conditions.

It is not sufficient to confess one's faults, to wish earnestly for fullness and to place oneself upon the altar. How frequently believers strive to do this, maintaining as long as possible such an attitude, without anything happening within them! Then, exhausted, they relapse into their previous state. They failed to take the last step, namely that of grasping through faith the blessing which God had already given them in principle.

Jesus Himself asserts this truth in the passage just quoted above, "If any man thirst let him come unto me and drink. He that believeth on me, as the Scripture hath said, out of his belly shall flow rivers of living water. But this spake he of the Spirit which they that believed on him were to receive" (John 7:37-39). Undoubtedly this passage refers not only to the Spirit but also to His fullness, for what finer image of overflowing fullness could we imagine than that of rivers of living water? If our hearts are to be so filled, the great and first step that we must take is to believe.

In this connection let us look more closely at the three stages through which our faith must travel.

a. Jesus Christ asks us first to believe in Him and to look to Him for everything.

So long as we place our trust in men or in ourselves, in our strivings toward goodness, our personal value or our experiences such as they are, we shall never achieve perfect freedom within ourselves. Our life and fullness are found in Jesus Christ alone. To be filled, we must discard all other things and look only to Him.

b. Once our gaze is concentrated on His person, Jesus Christ asks us to believe that He is in us through the Spirit.

We could claim to have in the heavens the most holy and almighty Saviour, but this would avail us nothing unless we also believed that He dwells in our hearts by faith. It has been constantly repeated that with the Saviour's spiritual presence we have all things; without His presence we are indeed destitute. Therefore the indwelling of the Spirit in our hearts is a vital truth.

c. We must believe that Christ fills us with His Spirit.

Because many Christians fail to complete this third stage for our faith they have never received fullness. This stage consists of opening wide our hearts to Jesus Christ, *meanwhile believing that He has filled us with His Spirit*. Innumerable believers have prayed over and over again to God, "Lord, fill me with Thy Spirit," and they have never received this fullness. Why? For the reason that they never laid hold, by faith, of that for which they asked. Mere asking for water will not quench thirst, nor will gazing at water once it is placed before one; it must be drunk, or, in other words, taken and appropriated to oneself. Fullness of the Spirit cannot be attained by ardent longing nor by mere request, nor by contemplation upon the fullness that is to be found in Christ; on reaching this point it must be grasped by an act of faith. We tend to think that we have to beseech God to fill us with His Spirit; it is He, on the contrary, who entreats us to believe and to discard all those obstacles which prevent His full possession of us.

When speaking of the Spirit's fullness, it is not by chance that Scripture twice uses the metaphor of drinking: "If any man thirst, let him come unto me and drink" (John 7:37), and "Be not drunken with wine, wherein is riot, but be filled with the Spirit" (Eph. 5:18). Man quenches his thirst by drinking deeply; we are filled by the Spirit and remain so by believing profoundly. In short the unbelief of many rests on these two points:

1. They do not think it possible that God could fill them now with the Spirit. Herein they limit His power and proclaim their ignorance of His injunction to make this a present-day experience.

2. Having prayed and yielded themselves to God, they dare not believe that they are filled with the Spirit because they do not feel it. Instead of starting with blind belief in the promise of the written Word they want primarily to feel and to see, and yet nothing happens within them. But Jesus says to us constantly, "Said I not unto thee that *if thou believest* thou shouldest see the glory of God?" (John 11:40).

Let us, therefore, start by *believing* and, in accordance with the promise in Scripture, rivers of living water shall surely flow from us, though (to ensure our continual humility) it is not always given to us to see them. Dr. Inwood in a pamphlet on the "fullness of the Spirit" declares, that in his opinion, the most critical moment for a believer desirous of being filled with the Spirit is the one which separates the instant in which he believed in this fullness from the instant when he sees the fruits of it in him and around him. But, as we shall see later on, if the Spirit fills us and we persevere in faith, this power will inevitably be revealed, though, understandably enough, in the form of His own choosing.

Finally, let us note that we receive the fullness of the Spirit, quite simply in similar fashion to other forms of spiritual grace. The just shall live by faith, and it is by faith that we are pardoned, regenerated, baptized, adopted, sealed and filled with the Spirit. When do we receive pardon? When we have long humbled ourselves, and cried incessantly to God, or spent years working for it? No, but rather in that instant when, taking God at His word, with hearts both contrite and yet assured, we believe that *we are pardoned.*

Following on from our full submission to Him, let us believe with humility and assurance that *we are now filled with the Spirit.*

VII. THE SPIRIT CAN INSTANTANEOUSLY FILL OUR HEARTS

Despite what we have just seen many people think that, though the fullness of the Spirit is ordained by God, it is however, impossible to obtain it instantaneously by an act of faith and that it takes a lifetime to attain it.

This would be true if the fact of being filled with the Spirit implied perfection. But it is not so; to the contrary, the Spirit's desire is to fill us as we are that He may lead us through the successive stages to perfection. Moreover we shall later see that the Spirit within us must increasingly fill us until we are filled with the whole fullness of God. This aim, which will be pursued during the whole of our life, will only be fully achieved in glory; nevertheless it remains true that the Spirit can and is desirous of filling us instantaneously, this very day, to the measure of our capacity. If, with this question in mind we study the Acts we note that the reception of the Spirit's fullness was instantaneous in each case mentioned in this book; on the Day of Pentecost the one hundred and twenty were all filled with the Spirit in that very moment when He descended upon them (Acts 2:4); the five thousand in chapter 4 were all filled with the Spirit as soon as they finished praying (4:31); lastly, Ananias was sent to Saul that the latter might be filled with the Holy Spirit (9:17). May we take courage and fulfill with God's strength the conditions He imposes upon us and, without further delay, we shall be filled with the Spirit.

VIII. MANY BELIEVERS, WITHOUT REALIZING IT, HAVE ALREADY BEEN FILLED WITH THE SPIRIT

The Lord speaking to the Church at Ephesus says, "I have this against thee that thou didst leave thy first love" (Rev. 2: 4). Have we not all known this first love at the outset of our Christian life? Naturally no reference is here made to a carnal and momentary passion, a sentimental flash in the pan with no future. A first love means a deep and sincere devotion binding our newly born soul to the Saviour. We possessed in our hearts an overflowing joy, perfect peace, a close communion with God and surprising strength in the face of temptation. Then it was easy to bear witness; prayer was the natural breathing of the soul, and Bible-reading provided us with a stimulus that remained ever fresh. Whence came this fullness of life? From the simple fact that our hearts, having yielded unreservedly, *were wholly filled with the Spirit.*

Then, alas, what happened to so many? Their zeal was cooled and the flame shortly died down. The new sacrifices asked of them grew too burdensome and they were drawn once again by the world's attractions. There were falls followed by discouragement and the "devoted thing" slid into their hearts; in short, their first love was cast away and the fullness of the Spirit (which they had, perhaps without knowing it) was lost. Of those who read these lines, is there one who has undergone this unhappy experience? Have you felt that you are now no longer what you previously were, that, as it were, a veil of sin separates you from God? Have sorrow and discontent taken possession of your heart, while you remain powerless and disappointed in your Christian life?

If this be your case, will you not ask for God's pardon for such retrogression and pray Him to fill you anew with His Spirit? He has promised never to cast out anyone who comes to Him in repentance. If you let Him purify you from your sins, if you yield yourself anew to Him, believing that you have within you the fullness of His Spirit, then, He will not only restore to you that first love which you lost but will give you more in increasing measure. For He is willing by His power working within us to do much more than we ask or think (Eph. 3:20). Lastly, let us recall to mind our Lord's words to him who has lost his first love: "Remember, therefore from whence thou art fallen, and repent, and do the first works, or else I will come to thee and will move thy candlestick out of its place except thou repent" (Rev. 2:5). Let us beware of resigning ourselves to a deficiency in our spiritual life, when full restoration is so royally offered to us. Such obstinacy will but lead to death.

It may seem contradictory that while we receive the fullness of the Spirit through faith, we can have this experience without realizing it. But the essential object of faith is now, and forever, Christ Himself. He who believes in Him, fully yielding to Him, can be filled with His Spirit despite ignorance of the working of the Spirit. But if he lack this knowledge he will not know what power he can depend upon, and this will surely hinder him in his spiritual life. On account of gaps in the existing teaching on the Holy Spirit, the number of such persons is greater than we imagine. Moreover, the same can be said in connection with new birth; it is received by faith and yet there are unenlightened people who do not realize that they are regenerated.

In conclusion we can say that such Christians ought not to consider the fullness of the Spirit as something new and extraordinary or impossible, but rather as a lost experience which they can recover and develop in this present time by following the path marked for them by God.

IX. THE FULLNESS OF THE SPIRIT CAN BE LOST BUT ALSO REGAINED

It is important to underline yet again what was stressed in the preceding paragraph; a child of God is not necessarily filled with the Spirit once and for all, or indeed forever. It is always possible for him to grieve the Spirit who, dwelling within him, respects his liberty. The slightest sin, consciously committed and not immediately confessed and abandoned, will lower the spiritual level. Straightway the Spirit ceases to occupy all and His living power no longer reveals itself as hitherto. It is obvious that a believer who is truly spiritual and filled with the Spirit will be more severely attacked by the adversary than a carnal Christian. He represents, in effect, a force which the enemy dreads above all else, and which he will seek to destroy even as officers in battle are first aimed at. Was not the Lord Jesus Christ tempted more than any of us? It is not by chance that the Epistle to the Ephesians (3:16-19; 5:18) having made mention of the fullness of the Spirit, goes on to exhort the believers to prepare for battle against evil spirits in heavenly places (6:10-17). The fullness of the Spirit can never become the pillow of sloth. It is, on the contrary, the indispensable equipment for that great fight and the great victory. May we here add (before dealing with the question further on in the chapter on "Sanctification through the Spirit") that this fight is won through faith and only by the power of the Spirit who reigns within us.

But what must a Christian do who has succumbed on some point, no matter what, and is in consequence no longer filled with the Spirit? Give way to discouragement, believing all his previous experiences to be irretrievably lost? No, indeed, for discouragement does not come from God. Let him recall to mind the promises of God's grace, and fulfill again those conditions upon which the fullness of the Spirit is always given or restored to us (see page 119).

a. Let him confess his fault and receive pardon and purification by the blood of the cross (I John 1:9).

b. Let him yield unreservedly to God the ground to which the Devil had been given access (Eph. 4:27).

c. Let him believe once again and then unceasingly that the Spirit, forever within him, fills his heart as much as and more than hitherto. The Book of Acts avers that it is possible to be filled with the Spirit more than once. The one hundred and twenty all received this fullness on the day of Pentecost (2:4). The majority of them (not to say all) were among the many disciples gathered together to welcome Peter and John on the first occasion of their liberation from prison, and they were, each and every one filled with the Spirit (4:31). Thus for some it was for the second time. May we, therefore, not fear if we perceive that we also need to be filled again with the Spirit, for that inexhaustible source of fullness is ever within our reach.

X. HOW DO WE RETAIN THE FULLNESS OF THE SPIRIT?

We have just noted that it is possible to lose and to regain the Spirit's fullness. But prevention is better than cure. The vital question is, How are we to maintain this spiritual level within us? It would seem that Scripture supplies us with the answer in two words (Rom. 8:4); we retain the fullness of the Spirit by walking:

> not after the flesh,
> but after the Spirit.

In the first place we must steadfastly turn our backs on all forms of evil, refusing admittance to the adversary, and beware of grieving the Spirit. Of course we shall never achieve this of ourselves, but the presence of Christ within us will give us the necessary power. Secondly, it is by living after the Spirit, submitting ourselves to His influence, His direction and His will, in short *by obeying Him* in all things, that we shall maintain our inward balance. (We shall return to this important question when dealing with "Sanctification through the Spirit" in the following chapter.)

XI. THE SPIRIT MUST FILL US INCREASINGLY EVERY DAY

In the spiritual realm failure to advance means retreat. We cannot therefore be satisfied with merely retaining what we have already received.

1. God desires to possess always more of us.

He desires that we should be conformed to the image of His Son (Rom. 8:29); we must all endeavor to attain unto full-grown manhood, unto the measure of the stature of the fullness of Christ and finally to be filled with the entire fullness of God (Eph. 4:13; 3:19). Yet Scripture succinctly declares that this absolute aim will be attained only in glory. When it shall be "made manifest what we shall be. . . . we shall be like him, for we shall see him even as he is" (I John 3:2). Only in His presence shall we be perfectly filled with the whole fullness of God. In consequence, therefore, I can never claim, here below, that I have received all that I can receive, that I have reached perfection and have no further progress to achieve. On the contrary, with my eyes fixed on the pattern before me, I must seek to become ever further filled with His life, to resemble Him more closely. This thought will keep me constantly poised and yet humble.

2. The fullness of the Spirit leads us to grow in our spiritual life.

New birth, by which we receive life, must be followed by constant growth. A carnal Christian is marked by lack of growth and a permanent state of infancy in Christ, unable to take anything stronger than milk (I Cor. 3:1-2). Conversely, the chief characteristic of a Christian filled with the Spirit lies in his possession of full spiritual health and concordant development to the end of his days here below.

It may be objected that this idea of growth stands in contradiction to that of the Spirit's fullness. But that is by no means so. A newborn child can have full health and physical vigor; nevertheless, he must and can, thanks to this vigor, develop until he reach full-grown manhood. His veins can be filled with blood and his lungs with air, but those quantities of blood and air will be insufficient for his adult needs. Similarly with a spiritual-minded Christian, God fills him according to his capacity and stage of development. Then, by the unimpeded action of the Spirit he will grow and be able to receive every day a yet greater measure of His fullness of which he will have need in face of new tasks and fresh battles. What sufficed him at the start of his spiritual life will no longer prove sufficient today, but, thanks be to God, he will never be able to exhaust the reserve of power and life which the Spirit is ever ready to accord him. F. Godet expressed it thus, "Man is a vessel destined to receive God; a vessel which must grow according to the measure wherewith it is filled, and be constantly filled to the measure of its growth."

Peter's example is striking. Twice we see him filled with the Spirit (Acts 2:4; 4:8). Consequent upon this experience and doubtless as a direct result, God reveals to him that on the question of Cornelius he is still full of Judaic prejudice which he must abandon (Acts 10:10-16). He obeys and thus takes a great step forward. Then later Peter, through human fallibility, commits a fault for which Paul sharply reproves him (Gal. 2:11, 14). This confirms what has already been said that man, though filled with the Spirit, can still sin; nevertheless he must and can grow spiritually by means of this very experience.

3. Increase of the Spirit's fullness within us will bring progressive victory over sin.

Scripture informs us that only in glory will we fully resemble Jesus Christ. It is sin which constantly hinders us from resembling Him; consequently, throughout our stay on earth, we must gain one victory after another over this terrible enemy. If it were otherwise, it would clearly imply that there was no further progress to be made. If, today, we are filled with the Spirit we shall conquer over all those sins of which we are conscious. But if, tomorrow, we continue to grow and advance on the path of sanctification, the Spirit will reveal to us further knowledge of ourselves, further duties to be accomplished and other sins of which, hitherto, we have been unaware.

Indeed, the more we progress in spiritual life, the greater our horizon becomes, the light grows stronger, our consciences more sensitive and we come to know the perversity of our own nature. If we remain in constant submission to the Spirit He will progressively give us the victory in all things, and we shall be able to pursue our way in the light, ceaselessly and increasingly filled with His presence.

One word more for those who, after gaining a real victory are discouraged by some new weakness or failure. We must not fail to remember that we remain for the whole of our lifetime in God's school. It is not surprising that a young student fails to grasp instantaneously, at the beginning of his schooling, all that he will be taught over a period of years. Despite the best will in the world we still make mistakes and are guilty of faults. But let us not be beaten by them, for if we remain submissive students, always eager to learn, the divine Master will unceasingly correct us, teaching and leading us from stage to stage to the attainment of the aim which He has assigned to us. We shall thus be preserved from two dangers: *discouragement* which may overwhelm us when we see, stretching before us, the road along which we must travel, and *pride* which may take possession of us as a result of our present experience of sanctification and fullness. Numerous, indeed, are those who worry little over their progress, saying, "We shall always remain sinners while on earth, and nothing that we do can alter this." They forget that without sanctification no man shall see the Lord (Heb. 12:14).

Others say, "I am now fully sanctified; for the past five, ten or twenty years I have no longer sinned." They only show that they have ceased to grow while believing themselves to have reached their ceiling, whereas in reality they have forgotten exhortations such as these, "Ye . . . shall be perfect, even as your heavenly Father is perfect," and "To him . . . that knoweth to do good and doeth it not, to him it is sin" (Matt. 5:48; James 4:17).

For our part, may we remember to aim at being "filled unto all the fullness of God" (Eph. 3:19), and let us say with Paul, "Not that I have already attained or am already made perfect; but I press on, if so be that I may apprehend that for which also I was apprehended by Christ Jesus" (Phil. 3:12). Then shall we be transformed into the image of Christ from glory to glory by the working of the Spirit of our Lord (II Cor. 3:18).

XII. WHAT ARE THE RESULTS ARISING FROM THE FULLNESS OF THE SPIRIT?

Once the Spirit reigns in us, possessing us entirely, He can then freely manifest His power and impart His life to us. This is implicit in Jesus Christ's words when He said, speaking of the Spirit, "He that believeth on me, . . . out of his belly shall flow rivers of living water" (John 7:38). To understand the results of the fullness of the Spirit, in their entirety, every field of the spiritual life must be taken into consideration, for there is none which will not come under His influence.

Like as an iron bar, black and cold, when placed in a furnace becomes glowing red through the penetrating heat, even so is our being penetrated by the presence of the Spirit. Let us, however, mention some of the blessings which He bestows on us according to the means of His fullness within us:

1. Abundant life.

That life in abundance, of which Jesus spoke, for He is the Spirit of life and through Him are we quickened (Rom. 8:2; John 6:63). When He holds undisputed possession of us He endues us, in place of a life that is narrow, weak, unprogressive, pitiful and sick, with one that is open, strong and filled with harmony, a life which in its development shines forth and transmits itself to others.

2. Sanctification.

He is the Holy Spirit who glorifies in us Jesus Christ, our sanctification. When He is paramount in our hearts He frees us from the law of sin and death, for where the Lord's Spirit is there also is liberty to be found (Rom. 8:2; II Cor. 3:17). He breaks chains asunder, brings freedom from slavery and nurtures within us the spiritual fruits of love, joy, peace, long-suffering, kindness, goodness, faithfulness, meekness and temperance (Gal. 5:22). He purifies us and exerts in us the power of attraction that the interest of others may be captured, but above all, He establishes between God and us perfect unity since He forever and increasingly eliminates all that would separate us from God.

3. Power.

Jesus said, "Ye shall receive power when the Holy Ghost is come upon you" (Acts 1:8). This power, once we no longer oppose it but are imbued with it, will fill us to overflowing; it will be revealed in the effectiveness of our service, in the faithfulness of our witness, as well as in our inward sanctification. It was through the power resulting from the fullness of the Spirit that Peter, on the day of Pentecost, brought three thousand people into the faith (Acts 2:41), and by this same power did the disciples achieve their amazing work recounted in the Book of Acts. This power is not given solely to achieve success but also to face trial and even martyrdom. If Stephen died victoriously praying for his executioners, it was because he was filled with the Spirit (Acts 7:55-60). Have we not great need of this power, both for our inner life and service and for our victory in the face of the trials and temptations that come with each new day?

4. Thanksgiving and praise.

It is striking that Paul, following on his exhortation to the Ephesians to be filled with the Spirit, should go on to enjoin them to speak "one to another in psalms and hymns and spiritual songs, singing and making melody with your heart to the Lord; giving thanks always for all things in the name of our Lord Jesus Christ" (Eph. 5:18-21). It does not come naturally to our spirit to praise God, thanking Him for all things, including trials and every sort of circumstance, even the most difficult. And yet what powerful means of triumphing have we in our hymns and grateful worship, wherein we confirm the victory of God! These we can maintain at all times and in all places only through the Spirit's fullness.

5. Perfect happiness.

Our Lord's promise, constantly renewed is that abundant life through the Spirit will fill our hearts with perfect satisfaction:

"Whosoever drinketh of the water that I shall give him shall never thirst, but the water that I shall give him shall become in him a well of water springing up into eternal life. . . . He that cometh to me shall not hunger, and he that believeth on me shall never thirst. . . . I came that they may have life and may have it abundantly" (John 4:14; 6:35; 10:10).

The principal aim of the Spirit's fullness is that God may be glorified in our lives; but how can we fail at the same time to experience great happiness, since God gives to us of His inexhaustible riches, and our hearts pour out ceaseless thanksgiving to Him?

CONCLUSION

Has not this chapter helped us to understand how imperative and possible it is that we should be filled with the Spirit? This blessing is the crown of that grace which God has bestowed on us through Jesus Christ. Without it we can spiritually vegetate and never carry out the full program with which God presents us. Let us, therefore, not disobey our Lord's explicit command and not push aside that supreme gift which He offers to us.

This is a most serious matter since a refusal on our part will lay us open to great danger. In this our age, more than ever, there is no place for those who are lukewarm. Those who have no desire to be on fire with zeal and wholly in God's possession will not be able to withstand the evil days which have been foretold. For even in the time of the apostles did Peter say to Ananias, "Why hath Satan filled thy heart to lie to the Holy Ghost?" (Acts 5:3).

To those who obstinately refuse to be won over and filled by God's Spirit will come one day, the dread realization that the adversary has taken complete possession of them. The prophets, speaking of the last days declare that in humanity's apostasy the enemy will increasingly find instruments delivered and dedicated to him. We who read these lines, do we not de-

sire to be members of that army of victors who will rise to hasten the return of their Master and will greet Him with gladness at His appearing?

CHAPTER 9

SANCTIFICATION THROUGH THE SPIRIT

I T IS JESUS CHRIST ALONE who was made unto us sanctification and in whom we become "saints" (I Cor. 1:30; Eph. 1:1). But it is through the Spirit, that is, His spiritual presence in us, that the Saviour sanctifies us. The New Testament uses more than once these following expressions, "sanctified by the Holy Ghost" (Rom. 15:16; I Cor. 6:11), or "sanctification of the Spirit" (II Thess. 2:13; I Peter 1:2). It has already been pointed out that sanctification takes place according to the measure wherewith the Spirit fills our hearts. We shall now see how this is brought about.

I. THE SPIRIT CONVEYS A NEW NATURE TO THE BELIEVER

Peter says that we become partakers of the divine nature (II Peter 1:4). Paul speaks on one occasion of "Christ in you," on another of "the Spirit in you," and on yet another of the "new man," to denote this new part of our being (Col. 1:27; I Cor. 6:19; Eph. 4:24). (The new man is not only man regenerated as we might be tempted to believe.) We receive this new nature at the very moment of our regeneration, and, as we noted in connection with the receiving of the Spirit, it is at that moment that He comes to take up His permanent abode in us. Let us take an illustration: a wild tree that produces nothing but bad fruit is grafted. It receives a new and superior nature which can, without effort, bear only good fruit. Even so, the Spirit imparts our second and new nature. Clearly the Holy Spirit cannot sin; thus if we allow Him freedom of action, He will bear in us nothing but good fruit. It was this that John expressed when he said, "Whosoever is begotten of God doeth no sin, because his seed [the new nature, the Spirit] abideth in him; and he cannot sin, because he is begotten of God" (I John 3:9). It is this seed of God, that which is begotten of God in him, which cannot sin and which becomes the instrument of victory.

II. THE OLD NATURE CONTINUES TO EXIST IN REGENER-ATED MAN

As the grafted tree retains its old nature, ever ready to re-assume the upper hand, so the believer will keep, right to the end, his old nature, the "flesh" and the "old man" in the words of Scripture. Confirmation of this is found, for example, in Romans 8, the chapter on victory, which does not cease to underline the conflict between the flesh and the Spirit in the believer's heart. No less than thirteen times is the word "flesh" mentioned in verses one to thirteen. Paul also urges the Galatians to "walk by the Spirit and ye shall not fulfill the lusts of the flesh. For the flesh lusteth against the Spirit and the Spirit against the flesh; for these are contrary one to the other, that ye may not do the things that ye would" (Gal. 5:16-17). Let us study more closely the Scripture's teaching on that "flesh" which continues to exist in us.

1. What, precisely, is the flesh?

The flesh is not solely the sin in us, what we consider to be bad in our personality, nor is it composed only of our body, our physical flesh. It is more than that; the flesh is our whole being, our SELF, all that we are by nature when not in Jesus Christ. It is Paul himself who gives us this definition: "For I know that in *me*, that is, in *my flesh*, dwelleth no good thing" (Rom. 7:18). Thus the new man is Christ in us through the Spirit and the old man consists of ourselves without Him.

2. The flesh is by very nature sold to sin.

"I am carnal, sold under sin," states Paul. "For I know that in me, that is, in my flesh, dwelleth no good thing.... I myself

... serve, with the flesh, the law of sin" (Rom. 7:14, 18, 25).
What man has not experienced his nature's inability to resist
sin?

3. This incurable flesh is unchanged in the believer.

As the old nature of the grafted tree remains wild, unable of
itself to bear anything but evil fruit, so the flesh in us "is not
subject to the law of God, neither indeed can it be" (Rom.
8:7). "The flesh lusteth against the Spirit, and the Spirit
against the flesh, for these are contrary one to the other; that ye
may not do the things that ye would. ... Now the works of the
flesh are manifest, which are these, fornication, uncleanness..."
(Gal. 5:17, 19, 20). Because of this unyielding opposition to
the Spirit on the part of the flesh, and its inability to be im-
proved or sanctified, God can do but one thing to free us from
t, namely, crucify it. We shall see later how this is brought
about.

4. It is possible for a believer to live after the flesh.

Paul's reiterated exhortations clearly mark such a possibility:
"For they that are after the flesh do mind the things of the
flesh. ... So then, brethren, we are debtors, not to the flesh to
live after the flesh. [We are under no obligation in this, but we
can do it.] ... If ye live after the flesh, ye must die ... Make
not provision for the flesh to fulfill the lusts thereof" (Rom.
8:5, 12, 13; 13:14). We also know what this same apostle
wrote to the Corinthians when he reproached them for being
carnal Christians and babes in Christ (I Cor. 3:1-3). And
lastly, on examination of our own consciences, we are forced to
confess that only too often we, too, have been carnal Christians.
Perhaps we are so still? If this be the case may we beware of
the grave consequences which such behavior entails.

5. "If ye live after the flesh ye must die ..."

We have already noted that those who knowingly and willfully continue to grieve the Spirit indefinitely by refusing to be
sanctified show that they are not truly born again and will ulti-

mately reach perdition. God's Word speaks plainly: "Follow after . . . sanctification without which no man shall see the Lord" (Heb. 12:14). Therefore let us awake and cry unto God, beseeching Him to deliver us from this body of death. This He will surely do if we are sincere, for He desires to give us the victory.

III. THE SPIRIT WITHIN US HAS THE POWER TO OVERRULE THE FLESH

1. "Where the Spirit of the Lord is, there is liberty" (II Cor. 3:17).

The Spirit is all-powerful and if we let Him act freely He will truly give us liberty. Following his description of the slavery of a carnal Christian seeking sanctification through his own endeavor, Paul exclaims, "The law of the Spirit of life in Christ Jesus made me free from the law of sin and of death" (Rom. 7:14-25; 8:2). Has He done it for us?

2. The basis of this victory was laid at the cross.

The Spirit only fulfills in us that which Christ won for us at Calvary. On the cross Jesus not only bore away our sins but also took with Him our "old man" and crucified him. He thus triumphed over our flesh, that root of all our sin which by our every effort we were unable to conquer or destroy. Herein lies the reason for Paul's declaration that "our old man" was crucified with Him that the body of sin might be done away, that so we should no longer be in bondage to sin; "for he that hath died is justified from sin" (Rom. 6:6-7). Nevertheless this crucifixion, carried out in principle is only fully realized in us through our consent and the constant working of the Spirit.

3. Through the Spirit we can keep the flesh in subjection.

Let us turn again to our illustration of the grafted tree. Through grafting the old nature was dethroned and made subject to the new. It finds subordination intolerable and, being the livelier of the two, it grows a number of shoots all as wild as itself. What will happen if the gardener does not keep constant watch and fails to lop off carefully these shoots? They will absorb all the sap, and the upper branches will cease to bear fruit until they finally die.

There is an exact parallel in us. If we are not on our guard the old man, always so lively in each of us, seeks to regain the upper hand. Left to ourselves we shall be defeated. But it is at this point that we must let the work of Christ be accomplished in us; if we yield ourselves to the Spirit, He will cut away all those evil shoots and will keep the old nature truly crucified. Because of this Paul says that now "we are debtors, not to the flesh to live after the flesh. . . . but if by the Spirit ye mortify the deeds of the body [the instrument of sin] ye shall live" (Rom. 8:12-13). Moreover he adds elsewhere, "Walk by the Spirit and ye shall not fulfill the lust of the flesh. . . . They that are of Christ Jesus have crucified the flesh with the passions and lusts thereof. If we live by the Spirit, by the Spirit let us also walk" (Gal. 5:16, 24, 25).

Finally, he expresses himself in this forthright fashion, "The law of the Spirit of life in Christ Jesus made me free from the law of sin and of death" (Rom. 8:2). By this he means to say that the Spirit, when granted freedom, will work in a manner as forcible and lasting as that formerly employed by sin when the flesh was all-powerful. Yet another example will help to illustrate this truth. If I take hold of my pen, its nature and weight remain unaltered. The law of gravity still has its effect on it and if I release my hold it will inevitably fall to the ground and be broken. What happens so long as I hold it? The law of life, which is in my hand, counterbalances the law of gravity and moreover enables me to use the pen which on its own is of no use. But if I relinquish it the object's own nature becomes paramount and it falls.

Similarly, when I yield myself to Jesus Christ, my "old man" remains unchanged; sin retains its hold over him and would attract him irresistibly if left to himself. But the power of the Spirit takes possession of me, insuring the continued crucifixion of the old man, and delivers me from the thraldom of evil. The working of the power, however, is proportionate to the measure of my will's submission to it. If I withdraw, my "old man" will rally and I shall have the unhappy experience of a fall.

4. Emancipation through the Spirit is progressive and not "eradication."

Some think that having once experienced sanctification, they can thenceforth sin no more; their "old man" exists no more, they say, and every root of sin has been plucked out of their heart forever. This might be called "entire sanctification" or "eradication." It is easy to see that there is no Scriptural authority for such a belief. Romans 6:6 does indeed state that our "old man" has been crucified with Christ, that the body of sin might be done away. But in the Greek, the words "done away" might be equally well translated as "rendered ineffective." Furthermore, chapters seven and eight of Romans show (as, alas, does experience) that the "old man" is frequently most active in the believer, and that sanctification is realized only in proportion to the measure of our submission and our faith. Our spiritual life must grow ceaselessly unto the measure of the stature of the fullness of Christ, and the Spirit must increasingly fill us unto the perfect fullness of God.

It is, therefore, obvious that up to the very end we shall have conquests to make and victories to win against sin, as has already been pointed out on page 131. Consequently, up to the last, we shall have to make sure that our "old man" is daily subjugated by the Spirit. Let him who thinks himself to be standing upright beware lest he fall. If we cease to exercise a constant watch on this point we run the serious risk of laying ourselves open to the crushing return to power of the flesh. To insist upon this is unnecessary as we have already too many examples of it before us.

IV. WHAT IS MAN'S PART IN SANCTIFICATION THROUGH THE SPIRIT?

This has been indicated more than once, namely, entire surrender of ourselves into God's hands, and the exercise of faith. It is, in fact, always the same, for every form of spiritual grace is received in similar fashion.

1. Surrender of the will into God's hands.

God can free me from sin and it is to this end that He places His Spirit in me. As soon as I no longer resist Him and surrender my own will, the Spirit fills and sanctifies me ever increasingly (Rom. 6:13). Nevertheless I remain free, but if my will ceases to be in submission then, immediately, the Spirit ceases His work. It must be further pointed out that such a halt in the Spirit's working is not brought about solely by an open act of rebellion of the will. It can be equally caused by that desire, that is so frequent, to fight with one's own power, seeking to manage one's own affairs without help, which is the characteristic mark of the carnal Christian. God intervenes to pardon, regenerate, and sanctify us only when we place ourselves in His hands that He alone might command, for He knows that no man will ever attain salvation and sanctification through his own endeavors.

Some perhaps will think, on reading these lines, that they do not possess sufficient strength of will to remain in constant submission to God. May they be reassured, for God asks for nothing more than a will that is truly sincere, regardless of its weakness. For the remainder, "it is God which worketh in you both to will and to work, for his good pleasure" (Phil. 2:13). It is enough that we leave the working out to Him. In this field, as in all others we can count on the help of the Holy Spirit. Our will may be weak or rebellious, but upheld by the Spirit it will become as reinforced concrete which, through its metal framework, has strength to resist all pressure.

2. Faith.

The just shall live by faith. As we receive pardon for our

sins by faith, so, too, by faith do we start out and progress along the path of sanctification (Rom. 6:11). Too long have we imagined that we could be sanctified by our own efforts, our strivings, our prayers and tears, in short by our own labors, and we have ended in failure. Let us leave this treacherous ground to establish ourselves on the rock of faith; let us turn our gaze away from ourselves to fasten it upon Him who is made unto us, wisdom, righteousness, sanctification and redemption (I Cor. 1:30).

The Gospels provide us with a wonderful illustration of victorious faith; Jesus, walking on the waters, was rejoining His disciples. Peter exclaimed, "Lord, if it be thou, bid me come unto thee upon the waters." And the Lord answered, "Come." What did Peter do? Did he start by tentatively feeling to see if he had become lighter than water? No, he knew he had not altered but he *believed* in the power of Jesus and went forth from the boat. While keeping his eyes on Him he walked upon the waters, but on seeing the strength of the wind he took fright and as he began to flounder he cried out saying, "Lord, save me!" And immediately Jesus stretched forth His hand and took hold of him and said unto him, "Oh, thou of little faith; wherefore didst thou doubt?" (Matt. 14:24-31).

Jesus also calls us to come out of our boat to walk with Him upon the waters of sin. Even if we answer His call our own nature will not be altered. How then can we walk without sinking? By keeping our gaze constantly on the Saviour, and then by faith we shall conquer our flesh and surrounding temptations. If, on the other hand, we look at our own weakness, at the adversary's strength, at the greatness of the dangers which surround us, we court disaster. But have we not, with Peter, a Saviour always close at hand, ready to stretch forth His hand to us? If we are sincere, He will know how to help us, during this apprenticeship of faith, to become conquerors and even more than conquerors.

A little further back mention was made of that progress in

sanctification which must be pursued by means of an attitude of faith throughout our existence here below. It only remains to underline the fact that this progress frequently springs from a definite act of faith and surrender which is a marking point in the believer's life and to which he never turns back. At the time of conversion we first exercised our faith by accepting pardon for all our past sins; since that day we have only persevered in that same attitude, receiving pardon for the sins of each day. So it is with sanctification. If, today, we yield ourselves unreservedly to be filled with the Spirit, and take the decisive step of receiving deliverance from sin through faith and not through works, we shall have effected a transaction the value of which we shall never call into question. Difficulties and fraility will still be ours, but we shall retain a basis on which to build.

V. WHAT ARE THE RESULTS OF SANCTIFICATION?

They are probably the same as those of the fullness of the Spirit already quoted on page 133. However, certain essential points should here be mentioned.

1. Sanctification bears in us the fruit of the Spirit.

When the flesh prevails over us the works of the flesh are made manifest in us; but when the Spirit triumphs He produces, effortlessly, all those virtues listed in Galatians 5:22, "love, joy, peace, longsuffering, kindness, goodness, faithfulness, meekness, temperance." He resembles the sap which rises and, by nature, causes the grapes to grow on the shoots attached to the vine-stock. What joy to be no longer sterile, in spite of so much vain striving, to witness with wonder the creative work of the Spirit!

The fruit of the Spirit is the very character of Jesus Christ placed within us. God has predestined us to be conformed to the image of His Son and He transforms us into this image from glory to glory through the Spirit (Rom. 8:29; II Cor. 3:18). The Spirit thus fulfills the Saviour's word: "The Comforter . . . shall glorify me, for he shall take of mine and shall declare it unto you" (John 16:14). How much we should thank God for this His desire toward us and humble ourselves at the realization of our unwillingness hitherto to let Him work in us.

2. Through sanctification we appreciate the justice of the law.

On account of the emphasis laid on the futility of attempting to gain justification and sanctification through personal effort, we may be tempted to forget that works must unquestionably follow the reception of these two forms of grace. Faith without works is dead, and a tree is always known by its fruit. If sanctification is for us only a doctrine, an intellectual theory, it can be of no value. The sanctification of the Bible is eminently practical; it produces works, otherwise it is nothing. Let us, therefore, beware of appearances of holiness, of Biblical phraseology and all pious attitudes which fail to correspond with our deeds.

We are, most certainly, freed from the law which can only condemn us. But once we have received, through the Spirit, Christ crucified and raised for us, we must put into practice all God's commandments, not in our own strength but in His, and not as an endeavor to gain sanctification, for He has already sanctified us by the Spirit. Paul expresses this truth in the following passage: "For the law of the Spirit of life in Christ Jesus made me free from the law of sin and of death. For what the law could not do, in that it was weak through the flesh, God sending his own Son in the likeness of sinful flesh and as an offering for sin, condemned sin in the flesh, *that the ordinance of the law might be fulfilled in us* who walk not after the flesh but after the Spirit" (Rom. 8:2-4). May God help us every day to show forth our sanctification through our works.

3. Sanctification by the Spirit refines our consciences.

The more we walk with the Spirit the more sensitive do we become to what will grieve Him. Our conscience, which formerly was asleep, becomes more alive and able to discern the voice of God. Sins which at one time were tacitly allowed will become abhorrent to it, and with each successive day we shall be able to discriminate more clearly between those actions which please God and those which displease Him. This is what Paul expresses when he writes: "I say the truth in Christ, I lie not, my conscience bearing witness with me in the Holy Ghost . . ." (Rom. 9:1).

On reaching the end of his life this same apostle realized better than ever before his natural state of perdition; and though, elsewhere he presented himself as an example of sanctified man (Phil. 3:17) he also wrote to Timothy: "Christ Jesus came into the world to save sinners; of whom I am the chief" (I Tim. 1:15). Many Christians, the more they progress in their spiritual life, are deeply perturbed by the increasing realization of the wickedness in their own hearts. They cry, "Though converted for many years I have never seen myself in such an evil light." There is no need to be downhearted provided, however, that through faith they lay hold of victory over each sin thus discovered. For the work of the Spirit is precisely that of bringing to our consciences deeper conviction of sin while ceaselessly fostering the development of the image of Jesus Christ in us.

4. Sanctification establishes an ever increasing communion between God and ourselves.

Sin separates us from God; sanctification, on the contrary, draws us closer to Him. "Blessed are the pure in heart; for they shall see God" (Matt. 5:8). Sanctification glorifies the Lord and admits us to close intimacy with Him. Jesus Christ said of his Father, "He hath not left me alone; for I do always the things that are pleasing to him," and for this very reason He could claim that God always answered His prayers (John 8:29; 11:42). God will surely honor us likewise according to the measure wherein our lives glorify Him.

5. Lastly, sanctification prepares us for the return of Jesus Christ.

On His return, the Saviour will take with Him only true believers, those who have oil in their lamps (symbol of the Holy Spirit). True believers will show that they are such by rising out of their momentary sleep and preparing themselves (Matt. 25:1-12). So too, when speaking of the Lord's return, Paul states, "Now it is high time for you to awake out of sleep; for now is salvation nearer to us than when we first believed. The night is far spent and the day is at hand; let us, therefore, cast off the works of darkness and let us put on the armor of light" (Rom. 13:11-12). And here, lastly, are the Lord's words in the Bible's closing chapter, "He that is filthy let him be made filthy still. ... and he that is holy let him be made holy still. Behold I come quickly and my reward is with me" (Rev. 22:11-12). If we would be unashamed at the judgment seat of Christ, let us hasten to be prepared by the Spirit's sanctification. Let us pray that God will awaken us and believers everywhere to our need of sanctification and cleansing "with the washing of water by the word" (Eph. 5:26).

CONCLUSION

Bearing in mind the points which have been mentioned let us examine our consciences and set ourselves certain personal questions: Are we dominated by the flesh or by the Spirit? Are we prepared to die with Christ that the old man may be truly crucified, and that we may walk in newness of life? Have we sufficient faith in the power of the Spirit who sets us free from the law of sin and of death? Are the fruits of the Spirit and the works of sanctification seen in us? Are we awake and ready for the return of Jesus Christ?

Lastly, may we never forget these two passages from Scripture: "Follow after . . . sanctification without which no man shall see the Lord" (Heb. 12:14), and "The God of peace himself sanctify you wholly; and may your spirit, and soul and body be preserved entire, without blame at the coming of our Lord Jesus Christ. Faithful is he that calleth you, who will also do it" (I Thess. 5:23-24).

CHAPTER 10

THE COMFORT, TEACHING AND GUIDANCE OF THE SPIRIT

WE TURN NOW, in this chapter, to the study of three new and particularly attractive aspects of the Spirit's work.

I. COMFORT

Four times in John, chapters 14-16, Jesus calls the Spirit "the Comforter." Who, indeed, unless it be the Spirit, working freely in us, could support us in our sorrows, receive us when discouraged, heal our wounds, dry our tears, give us quietness, kindle in our hearts a living hope and accord us peace which passes all understanding? Even in the Old Testament we read concerning the Spirit, "As the cattle that go down into the valley, the Spirit of the Lord caused them to rest; so didst thou lead thy people to make thyself a glorious name" (Isa. 63:14).

Paul wrote to the Romans, "Now the God of hope fill you with all joy and peace in believing, that ye may abound in hope, in the power of the Holy Ghost" (Rom. 15:13). Later when in prison and in the face of many trials the same apostle exclaimed, "I know that this shall turn to my salvation through your supplication and the supply of the Spirit of Jesus Christ" (Phil. 1:19).

Lastly, Peter makes this fine promise to those who suffer persecution for the sake of their faith: "If ye are reproached for the name of Christ blessed are ye; because the Spirit of glory and the Spirit of God resteth upon you" (I Peter 4:14). Was it not this that Stephen experienced when, at his martyrdom "he, being full of the Holy Ghost, looked up steadfastly into heaven and saw the glory of God" (Acts 7:55)? All this can be ours too, if we are willing to believe and be filled with the Spirit. How wretched are those who, in this world of grief, know not that unparalleled source of comfort, or who impede its soothing flow over their battered lives!

II. THE SPIRIT'S TEACHING

1. What is man's need of it?

Man left to himself cannot see the kingdom of God; he lies in spiritual death and the god of this age (world) has blinded his intelligence (John 3:3; II Cor. 4:4). The evil has invaded and perverted his whole being, not only his body and heart, his conscience and his will, but also his thoughts and his reason. God has revealed Himself to all men but they have turned away from Him through sin. "They . . . became vain in their reasoning, and their senseless heart was darkened. Professing themselves to be wise, they became fools . . ." (Rom. 1:21-22). Fools in the eyes of God, though they in their turn regard eternal truths as foolishness. "Now the natural man [i.e., unregenerated man] receiveth not the things of the Spirit, for they are foolishness unto him; and he cannot know them because they are spiritually judged" (I Cor. 2:14). The truth of this can be clearly seen in the present age: man despite his "sciences" flounders in the dark without the ability to solve any truly essential problem.

2. By what expressions is the Spirit's teaching promised to us?

God does not leave us in the dark if we are sincere. He gives to us His written revelation, His Word of truth, a lamp unto our feet and a light unto our path. Then, according to Jesus' promise, He teaches us through His Spirit: "The Comforter, even the Holy Spirit, whom the Father will send in my name, he shall teach you all things and bring to your remembrance all that I said unto you . . . when he, the Spirit of truth, is

come, he shall guide you into all the truth" (John 14:26;
16:13).

This work of the Spirit is of great importance and is in exact
keeping with His own rich nature. Indeed, is He not called the
Spirit of wisdom, of understanding, knowledge and truth (Isa.
11:2; John 14:17)? Having inspired the Scriptures He enables us to understand them and expounds to us the things that
pertain to God. "As it is written: Things which eye saw not
and ear heard not, and which entered not into the heart of man,
whatsoever things God prepared for them that love Him . . .
unto us God revealed them through the Spirit" (I Cor. 2:9-10).
Not only does He correct the conceptions of our spirit, warped
by sin, but also reveals to us heavenly truths beyond our imag-
ining. "And ye," writes John to the children of God, "have an
anointing from the Holy One and ye know all things. . . . And
as for you, the anointing which ye received of him abideth in
you, and ye need not that anyone teach you; but as his anointing teacheth you concerning all things and is true and is no lie,
and even as it taught you, abide ye in Him" (I John 2:20, 27).
This anointing, which is of the Spirit, we receive at the start of
our Christian life (see page 166).

3. What relation is there between the Spirit's teaching and
that of the Bible?

It is very understandable that we find ourselves in need of
the Spirit's teaching in addition to the written word of the
Bible. When we read with good natural eyesight the contents
of the Holy Book we can discover nothing without the aid of
light which comes to us from without and lights the printed
page. Similarly when, with the best will in the world we approach the sacred text our ignorance is such that, without the
Holy Spirit's illumination, we should understand nothing.
Herein lies the reason why so many unbelievers or people with
only a formal religion, have read the Bible and discovered
nothing in it. Indeed, the darkness of their understanding has
become more intense for Scripture is a living book which re-

mains closed to all those whose hearts are not set at rights, whereas to humble and sincere believers, to the "poor in spirit" who admit their ignorance, the Spirit's teaching is assured.

Moreover since the Spirit renders the Bible intelligible, it is in its holy pages, rather than elsewhere that He speaks to the soul. Of a truth where should we with certainty find His teaching if not in the Book which He inspired? "He shall guide," said Jesus, "into all the truth." But it is, precisely, His Word which is the truth and through it He desires to convey to us the treasures of His divine wisdom (John 16:13; 17:17). Our spirit is fallible and accepts, only too readily, the adversary's insinuations. Making notes of all the ideas which come to us, even though we may be honestly seeking God, will not bring us to the knowledge of the Spirit's teaching, but if we let the Lord speak to us through His Word we shall distinguish with increasing clarity the general direction of His will, and henceforth the Spirit will be able to guide us along that path in every detail of our daily life.

Note how often Scripture states that the Spirit will lead us into *all* truth and will teach us *all* things. It is not God's will that we should remain in ignorance, for if we fail to know the truth we cannot be set free from sin. Let us, therefore, hold this conviction that if we lack understanding of any wholesome truth or any Scriptural passage whose apprehension is necessary to us, the Spirit will grant it to us, in accordance with our needs provided that we humbly accept His tutelage.

4. The personal teaching of the Spirit is a characteristic of the New Covenant.

Under the Old Covenant, the priests alone had the charge of teaching the laws and ordinances of God to the people (Lev. 10:11; Deut. 33:10). But this is no longer so under the New Covenant: "For this is the covenant that I will make . . . saith the Lord; I will put my laws into their mind, and on their hearts also will I write them . . . and they shall not teach every man his fellow citizen and every man his brother, . . . for all

154 THE PERSON AND WORK OF THE HOLY SPIRIT

shall know me from the least to the greatest of them" (Heb.
8:10-11). Jesus, speaking of the New Covenant, also quoted
from Isaiah: "They shall all be taught of God" (John 6:45).
The Lord has achieved this through the Spirit.

Thus the Gospel teaches us that there is now no "laity" unable alone to grasp spiritual truths, nor is the "clergy" the sole
trustee of divine teaching. Peter and John pointed out that all
believers have been appointed by Christ to be "priests unto his
God and Father" and "a royal priesthood" (Rev. 1:6; I Peter
2:9). They "know all things" (I John 2:20) and all have
experience of the benefit of the Spirit's personal teaching. This,
however, does not prevent God from calling out certain men
to whom He grants special gifts, but they rank only as auxili-
aries, possessing no monopoly, and all other believers, called to
collaborate each in his own sphere, are members of equal foot-
ing with them in the same Body.

5. To what extent does the Spirit replace human teachers?

What, in fact does this passage mean: "Ye need not that
anyone teach you; but . . . his anointing teacheth you concerning all things" (I John 2:27)? It does not imply that we must
dispense with the ministry of those whom God has appointed
to teach His Church, or that we must ignore Paul's insistence
on "teaching and admonishing one another . . ." and his advice
to "exhort one another and build each other up, even as also
ye do" (Col. 3:16; I Thess. 5:11). For we are not saved to
remain in isolation, and a member detached from the Body will
perish. John's meaning is this: in the final analysis He that
teaches us and who alone brings light into our souls whether
through the direct speaking of the Word or by means of a
human ministry, is none other than the Holy Spirit. He is the
true Master on whose word we must depend and none of us,
not even the most ignorant, need yield servile allegiance to
human teachers, however great they may be.

Those who seek this, court unhappiness; since, passing from
one theory to another according to the fashion, always agree-

ing with the last speaker, uncertain as children and carried away by every wind of doctrine, they cannot know either that certainty or peace which bring rest to the soul; whereas all humble and submissive believers, who allow themselves to be taught by the Spirit and the Scriptures, can draw directly upon that source of unchanging truth. How magnificently does the Scripture herein proclaim the independence of the individual!

6. What particular teaching does the Spirit give in the midst of tribulation?

"When they shall deliver you up, be not anxious how or what ye shall speak; for it shall be given you in that hour what ye shall speak. For it is not ye that speak, but the Spirit of your Father that speaketh in you. . . . The Holy Spirit shall teach you in that very hour what ye ought to say. . . . Settle it, therefore, in your hearts, not to meditate beforehand how to answer; for I will give you a mouth and wisdom which all your adversaries shall not be able to withstand or to gainsay" (Matt. 10:19-20; Luke 12:12; 21:14-15). This promise was carried into effect quite literally for the Apostles and particularly for Stephen in the Book of Acts. How reassuring to know that it will be fulfilled for us too if we have to suffer persecution!

These passages have, at times, been abused by reading into them the implication that it is useless and even defiance to the Spirit to prepare oneself and meditate upon an address before attending a meeting, on the grounds that if one has to speak, the Spirit, in that very hour will teach one what to say. But as we have noted, the Lord reserves this promise essentially for times of persecution. It is indeed true that the Spirit in the course of a meeting can well give fresh inspiration to the speaker or urge someone to speak who had not previously thought of so doing. In this context we must be careful not to restrict the Spirit's liberty, or to turn this into a rule and thereby claim just excuse for ignoring any form of preparation would amount to setting a premium on idleness.

Moreover it can easily be seen that what is thus attributed to the Spirit consists frequently of nothing more than irritating repetition of the same, most elementary truths. Scripture, to the contrary, ceaselessly exhorts us, especially those of us that are acknowledged servants of God, to preparation and constant meditation in order that we may teach. Paul said to Timothy and then to Titus, "Give heed to reading, to exhortation, to teaching. . . . Be diligent in these things; give thyself wholly to them; that thy progress may be manifest unto all. Take heed to thyself and to thy teaching. Continue in these things; for in doing this thou shalt save both thyself and them that hear thee" (I Tim. 4:13-16). "And the things which thou hast heard from me . . . the same commit thou to faithful men who shall be able to teach others also" (II Tim. 2:2). "In all things showing thyself an example of good works; in thy doctrine showing uncorruptness, gravity, sound speech that cannot be condemned; that he that is of the contrary part may be ashamed, having no evil thing to say of us" (Titus 2:7-8).

Also to the Romans Paul writes, "He that teacheth [let him give himself] to his teaching" (12:7). And even in the Old Testament we read, "This book of the law shall not depart out of thy mouth, but thou shalt meditate therein day and night. . . . Blessed is the man that walketh not in the counsel of the wicked . . . but his delight is in the law of the Lord and in his law doth he meditate day and night" (Josh. 1:8; Psa. 1:1-2). If such advice were today followed by those who are required to speak, theirs would be the true teaching of the Spirit, and the flock, far from being undernourished would be truly fed with the Bread of life.

CONCLUSION

Are we conscious of the privileges which God confers on us through the Spirit? Let us never neglect the instructions of this divine Master, resolutely taking our place in His school through the constant study of His Word! So naturally and with such ease do we bind ourselves to a personality or a book from which we have derived some benefit with the consequence that we embrace all their ideas. Most certainly, let us be grateful for all the blessings which we have received by means of such men, but let us also daily search in the Scriptures to verify their words to us (Acts 17:11) and let us not be resigned to our ignorance which offends the Spirit of truth and is a hindrance to our sanctification. If we adhere to such an attitude we shall be kept from errors and preserve unimpaired that glorious liberty which belongs to the children of God, and our path will be lighted to the very end.

III. THE SPIRIT'S GUIDANCE

Not only does the Spirit bring understanding of eternal truths to every man, but also leads step by step those who place their trust in God.

1. When does the Spirit guide?

The Spirit guides us in a thousand different circumstances of life; in short He will guide us forever if we are prepared to follow Him. The Good Shepherd walks in front of His sheep, never abandoning them, and His Spirit leads them into all truth; that is to say, not only to the knowledge but also to the full realization of God's will. We have numerous examples of this in the Acts. While Philip walked near the Ethiopian's chariot the Spirit said to him, "Go near and join thyself to this chariot" (8:29). Peter was troubled by a vision which had appeared to him and did not know how to interpret it; the Spirit said to him, "Behold these men [sent by Cornelius] seek thee. But arise and get thee down and go with them nothing doubting, for I have sent them" (Acts 10:19-20).

Later, Barnabas and Paul were named and sent forth by the Spirit (Acts 13:2, 4). Then Paul and his companions were prevented by that same Spirit from entering various different provinces until they traveled into Macedonia (16:6-7). Finally at the time of his last voyage Paul stated, "Behold, I go bound in the Spirit to Jerusalem, not knowing the things that shall befall me there, save that the Holy Ghost testifieth unto me in every city saying that bonds and afflictions abide me" (20:22-23).

2. Whom does the Spirit lead?

Those instances of the Spirit's guidance just quoted concerned all God's servants. This is scarcely surprising, since, in the Early Church all were missionaries and "witnesses." But it is indeed to all believers who have received the Spirit that the promise is made: "For as many as are led by the Spirit of God, these are sons of God" (Rom. 8:14). This statement implies that all those who are sons of God are led by His Spirit. Paul, speaking to those who desire to walk with the Spirit, adds, "But if ye are led of the Spirit ye are not under the law" (Gal. 5:18). It seems superfluous to add that the Spirit's guidance is nowhere promised to those who are unconverted. How could the Spirit lead those who resist Him and prevent His entry into their hearts?

Is this not greatly reassuring for each of us who believe? We have this certainty that whenever the need arises God will reveal His will to us. We shall experience the realization of this promise, "Thine ears shall hear a word behind thee, saying, This is the way, walk ye in it; when ye turn to the right hand and when ye turn to the left" (Isa. 30:21).

3. How does the Spirit guide?

Normally the Spirit guides us by means of God's Word, as we have already seen. Undoubtedly, the Bible does not always mention the details of the facts that make up our daily life, but its general principles, illumined by the Spirit will be sufficient to guide us in a very great number of instances. For this, two things are necessary: first, that we should be steeped in the knowledge of the Scriptures by constant reading and study, for the light that God has so carefully given us in His Word, He will not reveal by any other means; secondly, that we seek, in prayer and meditation, to know His will concerning the particular case which is occupying our minds.

When Scripture fails to supply sufficiently clear guidance, the Spirit will lead us, always in the same way, by *circumstances*. Paul tells us that all things work together for good to those who love God (Rom. 8:28). There are, at times, combinations of circumstances which cannot fail to indicate a certain course. Our inner conviction will become so acute that there will be no cause for hesitation.

Alternatively, in order to guide us, the Spirit will quite simply use our sanctified *common sense*. It is imagined by some that to experience the Spirit's guidance it is absolutely necessary to hear a voice coming from Heaven, or to be the object of a supernatural intervention. No Biblical text gives grounds for such a belief and it would be dangerous to seek to imitate, at all costs, the cases mentioned in the Acts of the Apostles. Besides, in this very book, we read that at the conference in Jerusalem, the Early Church reached a decision, in a perfectly normal manner, on the serious question placed before it (whether the Gentiles were to be saved by faith or by adherence to the law). The disciples reasonably examined both sides of the question, made a note of the circumstances, quoted in its favor certain verses from Scripture, and then made a decision. Nothing miraculous took place, but this did not prevent them from declaring: "For it seemed good to the Holy Ghost and to us" (Acts 15:28).

The Spirit can also guide us in negative fashion, by *closing a door before us*. It is strange that, for many people, the Spirit's guidance always leads them to do *what they desire*. Very often, however, God opposes our desires, because He has something better in mind for us. To lead Paul to the evangelization of Europe, the Spirit is twice forced to prevent him from pursuing his own itinerary (Acts 16:6-7). Similarly, let us discern God's will when faced by a closed door, and may we not disobey Him by desiring to open the door despite God.

Finally, let us bear in mind that the Spirit can lead us, for our own good, *along the path of temptation and suffering.*

"And Jesus, full of the Holy Spirit, returned from the Jordan, and was led by the Spirit in the wilderness during forty days, being tempted of the devil" (Luke 4:1-2). The narrow way is not always easy, but it alone leads us to victory. Let us, therefore, be prepared to follow the Lord, wherever He may lead us; for if we die with Him we shall also reign with Him.

4. On what conditions will the Spirit thus guide us?

It would appear that the following are the chief conditions:

a. We must believe that God is guiding us.

"He is a rewarder of them that seek after him," and, "Without faith it is impossible to be well-pleasing unto him" (Heb. 11:6). Unless I yield myself to Him in faith, how can He lead me? But if I wait on Him and put Him to the test, He will most certainly carry out His promise.

b. Nothing must separate us from Him.

We have already made mention of the case of Achan. God led His people in the conquest of the land of Canaan, but as soon as sin, even a secret sin, crept in among the Israelites, He withdrew His support, and the people were lamentably beaten (Josh. 7). Similarly with us, God will lead us only while we are in full communion with Him.

c. We must renounce all self-will.

No one can serve two masters (Matt. 6:24). Unless we submit our will to Him, the Spirit will not guide us. Too often we act like people whose custom it is to ask for advice from those around them; we beseech God to reveal His will to us, then, in the moment of decision, we follow our own judgment. It is only after we have offered ourselves as a living, holy and pleasing sacrifice to God, without conforming to this present age, that we shall be able to discern His will (Rom. 12:1, 2).

d. We must also learn to wait.

God has promised to lead us in all things, but He retains the right to choose the moment for the intervention. How many characters in the Old Testament suffered painful experiences because of their impatience for God's revelation! Saul, for example, was on one occasion hard-pressed by the enemy; he had to launch into battle but he would not leave without first consulting the Lord. Samuel had not appeared, and the people were scattering; then Saul committed the sacrilege of offering up the burnt offering himself. As he concluded, Samuel arrived and proclaimed his punishment for such disobedience (I Sam. 13:5-14). We too are required to attend the school of patience, which should become for us a principle; so long as the Spirit's guidance remains indistinct, we must remain where we are (as did the Israelites in the desert), and continue to wait in trustful submission.

There may, however, come a time where waiting is no longer possible. By the circumstances the Spirit reveals to us that a decision must be taken immediately, but beyond that we have no further enlightenment. How shall we act with the certain knowledge that we are taking the right course? Time and time again such a case has been presented before us, and this is what we have done: having sounded the Scriptures and weighed the circumstances in prayer, we have said to God: "Lord, we wish to do Thy will and not ours; guide us. We consider this to be the best solution, and we are adhering to it. But if the decision we have taken is not pleasing to Thee, wilt Thou prevent us from carrying it out?" Then we have cast our burden on Him; if we have made the correct decision, He will let us act upon it; if not, so much the better, for He Himself closed the door and the situation became quite straightforward. And what joy to be able to say, on looking back, "The Lord was truly faithful to His promise; for in matters of both great and little importance, He has guided us!"

CONCLUSION

Is every reader of these lines convinced that the Spirit is ready to guide his life, even in the smallest details, to endow it with true happiness and to identify it with His will, always good, pleasing and perfect? May you, from this very day, have that experience. You will have but one regret, namely that of having failed to tread this path sooner.

In the Old Testament, we find an illustration of the way in which the Spirit enlightens and guides God's children. In the desert the Israelites were ceaselessly accompanied by the pillar of cloud. After the crossing of the Red Sea, it took its position between the Israelites and the Egyptians, protecting the former and lightening the night for them, while leaving the latter in darkness. Then it guided the people in all their wanderings until they entered into the Promised Land, not only deciding upon their itinerary, but also the exact moment of every departure and arrival (Exod. 14:19-20; Num. 9:15-23).

For this reason Paul makes allusion to it when he declares that the Israelites "were all baptized . . . in the cloud" (I Cor. 10:2). In our day the Spirit works in similar manner; He remains ever with us; He illumines the darkness which surrounds us, while concealing His light from God's enemies; He protects and guides us throughout our sojourn here below, and, if we possess patience, He will reveal step by step to us His divine will until we enter into Glory.

CHAPTER 11

THE HOLY SPIRIT AND
THE CHURCH

SO FAR, we have confined our study to the work of the Spirit in the heart of the individual. But we can make no further progress without dwelling on His work as a whole.

I. THE HOLY SPIRIT CONSTITUTES THE CHURCH

The Spirit not only regenerates those that believe, but also unites them to form the Body of Christ: "Christ . . . is the head of the Church . . . For in one Spirit were we all baptized into one body . . . Now ye are the body of Christ and severally members thereof" (Eph. 5:23; I Cor. 12:13-27). It was at Pentecost that the Church was founded. Christ died "not for the nation only, but that he might also gather together into one the children of God that are scattered abroad" (John 11: 52). Through the cross He reconciled men with God, and knit them together "that he might create in himself of the twain [Jews and Gentiles] one new man" (Eph. 2:15-16).

Then came the Spirit to baptize in the name of Jesus Christ the one hundred and twenty in the upper room, that with Him they might grow into one living Body. Thenceforward there have been no isolated believers, independent one of another, but members of one Body whose head is Christ. Starting from Pentecost, all those who become converted are united to that Body by the same experience of the Spirit's baptism (I Cor. 12:13). It is the Lord and not man who adds to the Church those who are saved (Acts 2:47). On the other hand, those who are not regenerated and have not received the Spirit cannot claim this membership and do not belong to Jesus Christ:

163

"Except a man be born of water and the Spirit, he cannot enter into the kingdom of God" (John 3:5). "If any man hath not the Spirit of Christ, he is none of his" (Rom. 8:9).

The Church, therefore, is not established by an organization, a government, human endeavor, or a particular doctrine. The Church is Christ, and all true believers of the New Covenant are united together by a living and indissoluble bond through the Spirit.

Do we belong to it? This is a most important question for, unless we form part of His Church, we cannot be saved. "And in none other [than Jesus] is there salvation, for neither is there any other name under heaven, that is given among men, whereby we must be saved" (Acts 4:12). And yet it is such an easy thing to accept the Saviour and become a member of His Body through faith.

II. THE HOLY SPIRIT ENSURES THE UNITY OF THE CHURCH

By definition, there is but one Church, for there is only one Head and one Body comprised of several members. "There is one body and one Spirit" (Eph. 4:4). In its bosom, unity is not created: it exists. "For as many of you as were baptized into Christ did put on Christ. There can be neither Jew nor Greek, there can be neither bond or free, there can be no male and female; for ye all are one man in Christ Jesus" (Gal. 3:27-28). If this were not so, the body could not live, for what would become of the members if they were separated from the Head or cut off one from the other? They would die. Therefore the Apostle urges believers "to keep the unity of the Spirit in the bond of peace" (Eph. 4:3). Their duty is to place themselves in Christ through faith, to ensure that they belong to His Body and that no sin separates them either from God or their fellow men; then, forthwith, unity, established by the Spirit, will be manifested.

Have we not each immediately felt the reality of this unity

when we happened to meet true children of God from another country or denomination? After a few moments spent in prayer or conversation on our mutual faith, we felt that we were standing together on common ground, and it seemed as if we had known them for a long while. There was between us, who had been strangers a few moments before, a fellowship of much greater depth than that which links us with our neighbor who has no share in our hope.

Note, furthermore, what has been so often said, namely that in the Body we find, not uniformity, but unity with diversity. The Spirit who created the body has also made each member differently that, being complementary one to another, they may find mutual support (I Cor. 12:12-26). This is most true when related to individuals who are variously gifted, but it is also true of groups of faithful Christians frequently endowed with special characteristics, which, nevertheless, prove useful to the Body as a whole.

The unity of the Spirit is, equally by definition, a spiritual unity. It is brought by Him in the hearts and consciences of those who belong to Christ, and is not the work of organization or of any government. Membership to a particular group does not necessarily establish unity which springs rather from the fact of general membership to Jesus Christ, our Saviour and God.

From the Epistle to the Ephesians (4:4-6) we learn what is the *immovable foundation* of the Spirit's unity. This foundation is composed of seven elements, which are:

1. One God and Father of all (v. 6).

We are united once we are in Him and He has become our Father.

2. One Lord (v. 5).

He is Jesus Christ as revealed to us in Scripture. He "is the true God" who offered Himself as "the propitiation for our sins, and not for our sins only, but also for the whole world" (I John 5:20; 2:2). It is impossible to have spiritual fellowship with those who do not believe in Him or His incarnation (II John 7-10).

3. One Spirit (v. 4).

All those who have received the Spirit are united by Him. It is in the whole Trinity that we are drawn together.

4. One faith (v. 5).

There is but one faith, founded on the Bible, inspired by the Spirit, and centered on the Son who came on the Father's behalf. This faith is marked by no inconstancy and it is totally incorrect to maintain that all beliefs and religions are equally sound. Therefore may we build up ourselves in our most holy faith (Jude 20).

5. One baptism (v. 5).

This is not baptism by water, concerning which there is such diversity of thought, but that of the Spirit whereby we are immersed in Christ and thanks to which there is neither Jew nor Greek, neither bond nor free (I Cor. 12:13).

6. One body (v. 4).

This is the Church, the Body of Christ, into which we enter through the baptism of the Spirit. Only in its bosom is unity to be found among the regenerated children of God.

7. One hope (v. 4).

Namely the return of Jesus and the consummation of our salvation. Indeed what truth is better able to unify us in an active expression of love and faith than the prospect of an early return of our heavenly Bridegroom?

It is easy to see to what degree these seven elements are essential. If one or other of them be wanting no real unity is possible; but if believers agree to accept them it would only be sin on their part that could prevent them from being united on such a basis.

Since unity is thus firmly established in Christ through the working of the Spirit and the will of God, we are greatly at fault for conserving it so poorly. If God's children really intend to spend eternity together it is high time that they start to be reconciled to one another in love here below. For our part we are convinced that the reconciliation, not external but deeply spiritual, which can be discerned on the earth among true believers is, beyond all question, a sign of the times. It would seem that God is preparing His faithful Church in view of His coming by an awakening of faith, a return to Biblical truth, by a truer sanctification and a greater demonstration of unity in the Spirit. But how backward we are still in comparison to what we should be!

Perhaps persecutions and difficulties will still be necessary to weld our hardened hearts together. Let us examine ourselves to see if we hold anything against one or more of our brothers in the faith, or if we sin by our attitude, our thoughts and feelings, our words or actions against the Body of Christ. May we bow in humility before God for any inconsistency of which we may have been guilty in this connection and He will then be able to bless us and use us to His service.

III. THE SPIRIT MAKES THE CHURCH HIS TEMPLE

We have seen that each individual believer is a temple of the Holy Spirit (I Cor. 6:19). But the redeemed as a whole form so many living stones which are built up to form "a spiritual house" (I Peter 2:5). "Ye are . . . built upon the foundation of the apostles and prophets, Jesus Christ himself being the chief corner stone . . . in whom ye also are builded together for a habitation of God in the Spirit" (Eph. 2:19, 20, 22). "What agreement hath the temple of God with idols? for we are a temple of the living God, even as God said, I will dwell in them and walk in them" (II Cor. 6:16).

These statements enable us to understand the privileges and holiness of the Church; but they also help us to estimate the duties of the Church toward Him who is pleased to place His presence in her. May we never fail to bear in mind that we are the temple of the living God and that no jealousy or meanness, no spite or worldliness, can be allowed in His holy abode.

IV. THE SPIRIT BESTOWS HIS GIFTS UPON THE CHURCH

In the body each member is so placed that it may exercise its proper function. In the Body of Christ the Spirit, with this end in view, gives a particular gift of His choosing to each member (I Cor. 12:11). (Further on we shall make a closer study of these gifts, page 180.) It is therefore the Spirit who enables the Church to work in the service of the living God. In Ephesians 4:11, 12 we learn that the gifts bestowed on the Church are sometimes the very men themselves whom the Spirit has qualified for the ministry. "He [Christ] gave some to be apostles and some prophets, and some evangelists; and some pastors and teachers, for the perfecting of the saints unto the work of ministering unto the building up of the body of Christ."

Fundamentally, all that contributes to the building of the Church comes from above, though man does have a part in the receiving of grace and in the service of God. There is here a close analogy to a newborn body whose members and organs were not formed by itself but created by its Author. Now all that God does is done well. If religious circles are frequently poor in gifts and qualified men, it is not His fault but that of man who hinders the blossoming of these gifts in others, or refuses to answer to the vocational call addressed to him personally. Let us give the Spirit the freedom to work in us and among us, for then will He immediately endow the Church with all these gifts that are so necessary to her.

V. THE SPIRIT GOVERNS THE CHURCH

The Book of Acts demonstrates this most clearly:

1. The Spirit calls the servants of God.

The Holy Spirit said, "Separate me Barnabas and Saul for the work whereunto I have called them" (Acts 13:2). "Take heed unto yourselves," said Paul to the elders at Ephesus, "and to all the flock, in which the Holy Ghost hath made you bishops to feed the Church of God, which he purchased with his own blood" (Acts 20:28). What a contrast would be seen if all those who seek to work in the present day were truly called and sent out by the Spirit! For whom God calls He also qualifies and He does not err in His choice of men or the distribution of the work.

2. He guides and upholds them in their ministry.

The Spirit not only prepares believers for the service of God by bestowing on them all His spiritual gifts, but also accompanies them step by step in the achievement of their allotted task, as we have already noted in our study of the way in which He guides the individual. "So they [Barnabas and Saul], being sent forth by the Holy Ghost, went down to Seleucia . . . But Elymas the sorcerer . . . withstood them, seeking to turn aside the proconsul from the faith. But . . . Paul, filled with the Holy Ghost, fastened his eyes on him," etc. (Following this intervention Elymas became blind and the proconsul believed [Acts 13:4, 8-9].) "Having been forbidden of the Holy Ghost to speak the word in Asia . . . they assayed to go into Bithynia, and the Spirit of Jesus suffered them not" (Acts 16: 6-7).

It was thus the early Christians made their conquest of the Roman Empire and that their efforts bore such fruit in abundance. Peter also could state, when speaking of them, that they "preached the gospel . . . by the Holy Ghost sent forth from heaven."

And who can say that the Spirit is not prepared to guide and help us today in similar manner, according to His good pleasure? May we not lack either faith or obedience.

3. The Spirit inspires the Church's decisions.

Jesus Christ promised the disciples that the Spirit would lead them into all truth (John 16:13). This promise was wonderfully fulfilled at the first conference at Jerusalem. Discussion had arisen among the Christians on a point of doctrine not then fully settled by the existing Scriptures (that is, whether the Gentiles were to be saved by observance of the law or by faith); they met together to examine the question and formulated their decision in these terms: "For it seemed good to the Holy Ghost and to us . . ."(Acts 15:28).

Of course, in our day, we are not called upon to settle such problems since we are in possession of the full revelation. But in all personal or collective decisions which we have to make, particularly in the service of the Lord, the Spirit's desire is to guide and lead us in a similar manner. Is not this what is lacking in our age when, over the smallest point which requires a solution, we indulge in interminable discussion, not forgetting to set up a commission or subcommission, while omitting only too frequently to seek for the Lord's counsel?

4. The Holy Spirit speaks to the Church.

Seven times do we find in Scripture this phrase, "He that hath an ear, let him hear what the Spirit saith to the churches," at the conclusion of each passage addressed by Jesus Christ to the churches in Asia (Rev. 2:7). And even now the Spirit speaks to the Church on the Lord's behalf, bringing messages of encouragement, of reproof, a call to repentance or to further work. This He does by underlining with suddenness and forcefulness a passage in Scripture or by imposing on a certain man the responsibility of acting as His spokesman; He still speaks through the measured voice of events or causes the still, small voice to be heard in moments of prayer. Yes, God has always something to say to us. May we have ears to hear what the Spirit says to the churches.

VI. THE SPIRIT SUPPLIES FOR THE CHURCH'S GROWTH

"So the church . . . had peace, being edified; and walking in the fear of the Lord, and in the comfort of the Holy Ghost, was multiplied" (Acts 9:31). This is easy to understand; the Spirit conveys to those who witness for Jesus Christ His power and wisdom, He convinces men of sin, regenerates them, makes them members of His Body causing them to grow in faith and sanctification. It is indeed by the assistance of the Spirit and not by human effort alone that the Church increases. This holds good for the present day; a greater number of workers, more abundant material resources, administrative reorganization, more frequent meetings and more urgent addresses will not of themselves bring an advance in the work, whose progress springs from the profound working of God's Spirit in all the members of the Body, who together hold themselves in submission to His will and faithful to His Word. May God grant us this for herein is a true awakening.

VII. CHRIST, THROUGH THE SPIRIT'S MINISTRY, IS FOREVER THE HEAD OF THE CHURCH

When stating, in accordance with the Scripture, that the Spirit establishes the Church, giving her unity, making her His temple by bestowing upon her His gifts, governing her and causing her to grow, we may perhaps be tempted to inquire what part is left to Jesus Christ. Let us not forget what has been mentioned already several times, that the Father, Son and Holy Spirit are One and that where one of the Persons of the Trinity is, the two other Persons are also present. Moreover the Spirit's role is not to speak of Himself but to glorify Christ (John 16:13-14). Far from superseding the Lord in the Body, He works for Him, gaining souls for Him, transforming them into His image, while conveying to the members life from the Head. Christ remains the supreme Head of the Church; it is He alone who is her Saviour, for He loved her and gave Himself up for her (Eph. 1:22-23; 5:25). Finally, it is to Christ that she will be eternally united for He will take her to be with Him, seating her beside Him on His throne.

In Genesis we can discern a very fine image of the Spirit's role. Eliezer, sent by Abraham, his master, traveled to a far country to seek a wife for Isaac, the heir to the divine promises. He meets the woman whose heart God had prepared; he talks to her, not of himself but of the bridegroom who awaits her, and bestows upon her magnificent presents as tokens of the riches and happiness which will soon be hers. Then he brings young Rebekah out of her native land to a distant country where the marriage is to be celebrated (Gen. 24). God, likewise, sends His Spirit into the world today to seek and prepare the Church, His Son's Bride. The Spirit captures Her heart by speaking to her, not of Himself but of her divine Bridegroom; He decks her with His gifts which are a token of future glory and heavenly joy. Then, once she is ready He carries her away to meet the Lord that the marriage of the Lamb may be celebrated.

Part IV

THE HOLY SPIRIT AND SERVICE

CHAPTER 1

THE ANOINTING OF THE HOLY SPIRIT

WITHOUT THE SPIRIT, by whom we are quickened and sanctified, we cannot possess eternal life. Quite clearly, moreover, without Him we cannot serve God, for it is only from the Spirit that we derive the necessary power. Jesus was referring to the Spirit when He said, "He that believeth on me, the works that I do, shall he do also, and greater works than these shall he do, because I go to the Father. . . . And I will pray the Father and he shall give you another Comforter" (John 14:12, 16). Peter was the first to experience the fulfillment of these words on the day of Pentecost. Being filled with the Spirit, he led on a single occasion, through one address, three thousand persons into the faith, a result never achieved by Christ throughout the whole of His ministry on earth (Acts 2:41). Let us therefore inquire what is the Spirit's part in connection with our service.

The Scripture distinctly states that we are anointed with the Spirit: "Now he that stablisheth us with you in Christ, and *anointed us,* is God; who also sealed us and gave us the earnest of the Spirit in our hearts" (II Cor. 1:21-22). "Ye have an anointing from the Holy One and ye know all things . . . And as for you, the anointing which ye received of him abideth in you, and ye need not that anyone teach you" (I John 2:20-27).

I. WHAT DOES THIS ANOINTING SIGNIFY?

We have the necessary clue in the Old Testament in the illustration of the oil of anointing which stands as a symbol of the

175

Spirit. Under the old covenant the following were anointed with oil:

1. The priests.

God said to Moses, concerning Aaron and his sons: "Thou ... shalt anoint them and consecrate them and sanctify them, that they may minister unto me in the priest's office. ... Thou shalt anoint him [Aaron] ... and thou shalt anoint them [his sons]; and thou shalt anoint them, as thou didst anoint their father, that they may minister unto me in the priest's office; and their anointing shall be to them for an everlasting priesthood throughout their generations" (Exod. 28:41; 40:13-15).

2. The kings.

Saul, David, Solomon, etc., were each consecrated as kings by being anointed with oil (I Sam. 10:1; I Kings 1:39).

3. The prophets.

Elisha, for example, was anointed by Elijah to be a prophet in the latter's place (I Kings 19:16).

Each of these examples is equally applicable to the believers of the New Covenant. Clearly enough, Christ alone is the High Priest and King of kings, and because of these titles He has received the Spirit's anointing beyond measure (see pages 41–42); we also are kings and priests with Him (I Peter 2: 9; Rev. 1:6) and we share His anointing even as the sons of Aaron shared that of their father. In truth, are we not called to reign with Christ and from now on to represent God before men even as we represent men to God through our intercession? We also are God's witnesses carrying the word of life as did the prophets under the Old Covenant. Like them, we stand in need of investiture from on High.

II. WHAT DOES THIS ANOINTING IMPART TO US?

The passages quoted above indicate quite clearly that through anointing we are set apart in consecration to the service of God. Anointing with the Spirit is therefore an indispensable *preparation* in face of the task which has been entrusted to us. By this preparation we receive the necessary power to accomplish it, even as Jesus Christ was anointed with the Spirit and with power at the outset of His ministry (Acts 10:38). By it we also obtain the *wisdom* and understanding of which we stand in need: "As for you, the anointing which ye received of him abideth in you and ye need not that anyone teach you; but as his anointing teacheth you concerning all things, and is true and is no lie, and even as it taught you, abide ye in him" (I John 2:27).

Two points arise out of this passage: (a) it is to all, and not merely to a privileged few that spiritual understanding is given; (b) the essential preparation for the ministry consists of being anointed and taught by the Holy Spirit who leads us into all truth. No human master, no school, can ever replace Him; and indeed we never risk preparing ourselves overmuch, both intellectually and spiritually in face of the responsibilities with which God desires to entrust us.

But let us bear in mind that study, knowledge and understanding itself, unless they have their origin in the Holy Spirit, will be infinitely harmful both for us and those around us. Furthermore, the divine anointing does not, as it is too often thought, exclude both work and research. It has already been pointed out that the Bible says to us constantly: "Meditate therein day and night . . . Be diligent in these things . . . Seek . . . and ye shall find." We are never encouraged to be idle through the anointing. May we profit by all the means given to us to learn and perfect ourselves for our particular ministry; but let us remember, no matter if we rank among the most ignorant of men, that in Christ alone are hidden the treasures of wisdom and knowledge (Col. 2:3) and that they are revealed to us by the Spirit.

Lastly, anointing brings us that radiance and infectious joy, without which our ministry will lack appeal. Psalm 45:7 says of Christ, "Therefore God, thy God, hath anointed thee with the oil of gladness." The Psalmist also exclaims, "Thou hast anointed my head with oil and my cup runneth over" (Psa. 23:5); and "My horn hast thou exalted, like the horn of the wild ox; I am anointed with fresh oil" (Psa. 92:10). In truth, oil does make the face to shine radiantly. If our own person were always lovable, joyful and appealing, how much easier and fruitful our service for God would become!

III. WHEN AND HOW DO WE RECEIVE THE SPIRIT'S ANOINTING?

Does God grant it to us after long years of Christian living in which we have given proof of our ability and worthiness to serve Him? No, indeed. This grace is contained, along with many others, in the *gift* of the Spirit whom we receive at the time of regeneration by accepting the Saviour. God bestows this grace upon each of us to make us able to serve Him, even before we set ourselves to this task. In the Old Testament we noted that the priests, kings and prophets were anointed before their ministry began, in order that they might be able to pursue it. Let us not be so foolish as to attempt to do without it. If we still lack it, what must we do to receive it? Quite simply, accept Jesus Christ through faith; He will save us, give us the Holy Spirit and forthwith anoint us for His service. Without Him we can do nothing, and, moreover, since Jesus Christ Himself had need of anointing, and as God now grants it to all (I John 2:20), none of us has the right to declare himself unable to serve Him; indeed to do this, would be to offend the divine Master by scorning the power and ability which He would impart to us.

We believe that it is needful to make a distinction between the Spirit's anointing which God grants to all His children at the first moment of belief, and the power with which He specially invests certain of His servants. It has happened that some great men of God have had to undergo a long preparation, through suffering, strife and prayer, for a special task with which God wished to entrust them. Moses' face, for example,

began to shine in the eyes of all the people of Israel after he
had twice spent forty days on the mountain in close communion with God, foregoing both food and drink (Exod. 34:
28-29; Deut. 9:9, 18). It is by the death of our Self and an
increasingly closer communion with the Lord that the Spirit can
convey to us His power. Clearly this occurs through faith,
though it is not always unaccompanied by a struggle with Self.
In what concerns us, we must not seek to copy the experiences
of another, whoever he may be, for each receives a special voca-
tion from the Sovereign Lord.

If we fully yield ourselves into His hands and are prepared
to pay any price required, He will truly show us the way in
which He desires us to experience, through the Spirit, the infinite greatness of His power, and will anoint us afresh for every
new task presented to us.

CHAPTER 2
THE GIFTS OF THE SPIRIT

GENERAL

I. WHAT IS A GIFT OF THE SPIRIT OR A SPIRITUAL GIFT?

IT IS A CERTAIN QUALIFICATION given by the Spirit to each individual believer to enable him to serve within the framework of the body of Christ.

Paul explains this for us by using the illustration of the body with all its different members (I Cor. 12). The body is one and yet it has a variety of members which are all indispensable, for each one of them serves in a capacity that is complementary to the functions of the remainder. Similarly in the case of believers: they form the Body of Christ with its members, each with its appointed task; from the Spirit each receives the particular gift relevant to his function (I Cor. 12:27, 11).

II. WHAT ARE THE DIFFERENT SPIRITUAL GIFTS?

It must first be stated that the Spirit is one and that all believers receive the same Spirit without distinction. But the Spirit who calls us to various fields of service, bestows the following diversity of gifts (I Cor. 12:4, 8-10, 28).

1. The gift of wisdom (v. 8)
2. The gift of knowledge (v. 8)
3. The gift of faith (v. 9)
4. The gift of healing (v. 9)
5. The gift of the working of miracles (v. 10)
6. The gift of prophecy (v. 10)
7. The gift of the discerning of spirits (v. 10)

180

8. The gift of tongues (v. 10)
9. The gift of the interpretation of tongues (v. 10)
10. The gift of apostleship (v. 28)
11. The gift of teaching (v. 28)
12. The gift of giving assistance (v. 28)
13. The gift of governing (v. 28)

And elsewhere we find:

14. The gift of being evangelists (Eph. 4:11)
15. The gift of being pastors (Eph. 4:11)
16. The gift of liberality (Rom. 12:8)

It may well be that mention is to be found elsewhere of other gifts, for no claim is made that the above list is complete. Whatever be the task to which God has called us, He will immediately give us, through the Spirit, the necessary qualification.

III. WHO CHOOSES THE GIFT THAT WE ARE TO RECEIVE?

Since it is written "desire earnestly the greater gifts" (I Cor. 12:31), can I stop at the choice of one that pleases me most and say to God: "Lord, I want at all costs this particular gift. I shall fight, strive and hope for it until I receive it"? Many have so acted and become discouraged (if they did not lose faith altogether) because their desire was not granted. If it was left entirely to our choice, would we not, for example, all like to govern? Is not the ministry of the Word so generally appealing that, if believers are not called to speak in the Church, they think that there is nothing left for them to do? If every member of the body were a mouth, what a fearful cacophony of sound would result! No, it is God alone, through the Spirit, who by virtue of His sovereignty, decides upon the qualification of which we stand in need for a ministry which He alone foresees: "But all these worketh the one and the same Spirit, dividing to each one severally *even as he will*" (I Cor. 12:11). Hebrews 2:4 also speaks of the Holy Spirit's gifts as distributed "according to his own will." If we place ourselves entirely at God's disposal, He will surely reveal to us the task with which He desires to entrust us and will grant us the necessary gift whereby to accomplish it.

IV. EACH CHILD OF GOD IS GIVEN A GIFT

In the body, there are no useless members or organs. In the Body of Christ, each believer receives a gift to carry out the function allotted to him. "There are diversities of workings, but the same God, who worketh all things in *all*. But to *each one* is given the manifestation of the Spirit . . . but all these worketh the one and same Spirit, dividing to *each one* severally even as he will . . . Now ye are the body of Christ, and members *each* in his part" (I Cor. 12:6-7, 11, 27, R.V. marg.).

What a privilege to know that by God's grace we can be of some particular service! And that the Lord, and indeed the Church too, have need of us! To the most humble of believers, to the most illiterate, to the youngest convert, the Holy Spirit grants a gift. Do you know which is yours? If you do not know, the reason is probably because you have never put yourself at God's disposal and have not allowed Him to indicate to you where and how He desires to employ you. Will you not today rectify this fault and ask God to use you in His cause? He will show you what you should do, and that gift which is marked for you will be revealed and developed of itself, through your obedience.

Note yet once again that it is of no consequence if you do not possess one of those gifts listed in section II, provided that you have a gift, even a hidden one, given to you of God. But make certain that you are not a parasite or a paralyzed member of the Body of Christ.

V. BELIEVERS DO NOT ALL RECEIVE THE SAME GIFT

In the first place, an individual does not receive all the gifts at the same time, even as in the body, the eye, the ear, the hand do not fulfill more than one function. "For to one is given, through the Spirit, the word of wisdom, and to another the word of knowledge . . . to another faith" (I Cor. 12:8-10). "For even as we have many members in one body and all the members have not the same office, so we, who are many, are one body in Christ, and severally members one of another. And having gifts differing according to the grace" (Rom. 12:4-6).

It follows therefore that we cannot expect to receive a certain gift merely because others around us possess it. If we do not each receive every gift, it is equally obvious that we do not all receive the same gifts: "Are all apostles? Are all prophets? Are all teachers?" (I Cor. 12:29-30). May we therefore learn first to remain humble and contented with the gift that has been given us, whatever it may be; and secondly not to covet the gifts that others have, but rather to seek for personal discernment of God's will and to wait on Him for all things.

VI. DO SOME GIFTS CARRY GREATER IMPORTANCE THAN OTHERS?

Yes, because Paul in listing them says: "God hath set some in the Church, first apostles, secondly prophets, thirdly teachers" (I Cor. 12:28). This would seem to establish a degree of importance among the various gifts. This is further apparent when he compares the gift of tongues with that of prophecy which he ranks above the former. "Now I would have you all speak with tongues, but rather that ye should prophesy: and greater is he that prophesieth than he that speaketh with tongues, except he interpret. . . . I had rather speak five words with my understanding, that I might instruct others also, than ten thousand words in a tongue" (I Cor. 14:5, 19).

VII. ARE SPIRITUAL GIFTS GIVEN IN ALL AGES ALIKE?

Often believers have been troubled by the fact that miraculous gifts, which were so abundant in the time of the Apostles, are so infrequently met with in our age, and many have believed that if our faith were greater we also should see the same supernatural power at work again. It is quite obvious

that the power of God has not changed, and that if we were
in closer communion with Him, this power would reveal itself
more strongly on our behalf. But close examination of the
Bible leads us to these two following conclusions:

a. If we look down the list of spiritual gifts, we note that
the majority of them (wisdom, understanding, faith; evangelists, teachers, pastors; government, assistance, liberality, etc.)
has at all times been granted to the faithful according to their
faith; and yet these are as supernatural as those gifts which
are called "miraculous," since they all come from the Holy
Spirit. If "miraculous" gifts (healing, miracles, prophecy,
tongues) have been absent at certain times, the probable cause
has lain not always in man's unbelief, but in the will of God.
If it were otherwise, why should the Spirit unceasingly give
certain gifts (quoted by Paul at the head of his list) while failing to bestow others?

b. In the Old as in the New Testament, God increased the
number of miracles at certain given moments, for reasons which
are easily recognized. When He called the Israelites out of
Egypt to make them His people, and again when He gave them
His law at Sinai and led them into Palestine, He performed
through His servants certain extraordinary signs, thus furnish-
ing proof both of His intervention, and of the supernatural
origin of the Old Covenant. Then miracles ceased for many
centuries only to become frequent again during the ministry of
Elijah and Elisha, a period marked not by spiritual awakening
but by infidelity. Great men of God such as Abraham, David,
John the Baptist, performed no miracles to the best of our
knowledge, and yet their absence was not due to lack of belief,
because John the Baptist, for example, was declared to be the
greatest of them all (Matt. 11:11; John 10:41).

Again in the Gospels and in Acts, numerous miracles accompanied the founding of the New Covenant, testifying to the
divine origin of the message proclaimed by Christ and the
Apostles. They were indispensable to convince the religious

Jews bound to the Mosaic law, and those who could then have had no other proof of the truth of the Gospel. This is the primary meaning of the words of Jesus: "These signs shall follow them that believe; in my name shall they cast out devils, they shall speak with new tongues, they shall take up serpents; and if they drink any deadly thing, it shall in no wise hurt them; they shall lay hands on the sick and they shall recover" (Mark 16:17-18). All these miracles (except that of poisonous drink) are to be found in the Acts, but nowhere in the Epistles, which form a fully defined statement of the laws of spiritual life, are we given to understand that in the present dispensation they are the indispensable adjunct of preaching and of faith. Passages such as Romans 15:19; II Corinthians 12:12, and Hebrews 2:3-4 would seem to refer to historical signs performed by the Apostles to support the original proclamation of the Gospel.

If such signs are today reproduced largely in mission fields, it is because the situation there closely resembles that prevalent in the Roman world, nineteen centuries ago. In our countries, where the Gospel has been preached for some considerable time, knowledge of the New Testament, together with the history of the faithful Church and the actual presence of a host of true believers, provides any honest soul with new and irrefutable proofs. Thus, from this point of view, miracles are now not so indispensable as they were in the days of the Early Church. Of course, God is almighty and it is for Him to decide if He wishes to give the same signs or the same gifts as in times past.

It is, however, arresting to note that Scripture, speaking of the last days, makes persistent reference to miracles performed not by God and those that are His, but by the adversary and his myrmidons. "For there shall arise false Christs and false prophets, and shall show great signs and wonders, so as to lead astray, if possible, even the elect" (Matt. 24:24). "Even he, whose coming is according to the working of Satan with all power and signs and lying wonders, and with all deceit of un-righteousness for them that are perishing, because they received not the love of the truth that they might be saved" (II Thess. 2:9-10). The false prophet "doeth great signs . . . and he de-ceiveth them that dwell on the earth by reason of the signs which it was given him to do in the sight of the beast" (Rev. 13:13-14).

Let us therefore be on our guard. While forebearing to limit the expression of God's power by our incredulity or lack of obedience, let us bear in mind that there are miracles and spir-itual gifts counterfeited by the enemy of our souls and that, in our day preceding the anticipated return of Christ, these coun-terfeits will become more and more numerous. Already Spir-itism, Science (self-styled Christian), Buddhism and many other movements, certain of which have nothing in common with the Gospel, do miracles, heal the sick, prophesy and speak with tongues. Perfect submission to God's Spirit and to *His whole Word* alone can save us from error.

VIII. ARE THE GIFTS OF THE SPIRIT ALWAYS A GUARANTEE OF GREAT SPIRITUALITY?

Alas, no! Strange as it may seem, it is possible to possess certain spiritual gifts and yet advance but little on the path of sanctification. Paul wrote to the Corinthians that they lacked no gift and implied that the gift of tongues was common among them; yet he added that they were still carnal, children in Christ and unable to bear strong meat (I Cor. 1:7; 14; 3: 1-3). We can, in part, see an analogy to this in our age which craves for sensations and enjoyment even in the field of re-ligion; it is not the most spiritual among gifts that are sought after, but rather those that appeal to the senses, that bring physi-cal advantage and which give rise to ecstasies and make much of feelings. Too often this worldly search loses from sight the necessity of sanctification "without which no man shall see the Lord" (Heb. 12:14). Yet Scripture distinctly states that any

If there is any field in which the adversary seeks to produce false miracles, of which mention was made earlier, it is most certainly in that of healings. Those movements which most stand in opposition to the Gospel have their healers and frequently undeniable miracles. Even in circles where appeal is made to the Bible, one witnesses today a mechanical approach to healings, which recalls to mind this passage: "Lay hands hastily on no man" (I Tim. 5:22).

Moreover, the method employed strangely resembles that used by hypnotists: why, instead of placing the hands flat on the head, does the healer rub the back of the head where the nerve centers are to be found? Lastly, it is easily established that a great number of patients who have received the laying on of hands, return ten or even a hundred times to receive it anew before finding relief, if indeed they ever find it. If it were truly the Biblical gift of healing, such as the apostles practiced, these persons would be healed at the first imposition; for in every case of miracles and healings mentioned in the Gospels and in the Acts, the results were achieved instantaneously (even with the blind man of Bethsaida, who was immediately healed by Jesus, in two stages [Mark 8:22-26]).

III. THE GIFT OF PROPHECY

I Corinthians 12:10. This gift does not solely convey the faculty of foretelling the future, but also, according to the definition found in I Corinthians 14:3-4, that of edifying, exhorting and comforting. Indeed, apart from the prophecies already contained in the Bible and the words of Jesus, we have in the New Testament very few examples of the future being foretold. The most striking of these is that of Agabus who announced beforehand a great famine which occurred in the days of Claudius, and who predicted to Paul what would happen to him in Jerusalem (Acts 11:27-28; 21:10-11). It would seem that, in the Early Church, the practice of the gift of prophecy consisted more often in the delivery of an inspired message or some revelation for the purpose of instructing and edifying the Church in the course of general meetings (I Cor. 14:3-4, 24, 29-33).

As the human mind will readily accept its own thoughts as divine inspirations, the rule was that every prophecy had to be judged and controlled by the other prophets (vv. 29, 32). It is easily understood why this gift was so highly thought of among the first Christians, and why Paul urged them to seek it more than others (v. 1). At that time, they did not possess the New Testament and had not always among them an apostle who was able to give them reliable teaching. It was the duty of prophets to feed the faith of the believers by sure revelation of gospel truths. But since the completion of the Bible, wherein the divine revelation is given to us once and for always, the gift of prophecy is not so necessary as it was at the start of the Christian era. Of a truth, it is often identical with the gift of exhortation or powerful preaching based on God's Word.

Some today claim to possess the gift of prophecy as held in the Early Church. They go into a form of trance and start to speak as if they were God Himself: "I, the Lord, declare . . . I announce . . . Do this . . . , etc." Clearly, God has the power today to claim a man and to speak through his mouth as He did formerly. However, when these prophets are mistaken, contradict one another, and deliver messages which are decidedly inferior to Biblical revelation, or even to an ordinary sermon (which, alas, is heard only too frequently), we are forced to conclude that herein too counterfeit insinuates itself, and we are led to hold ourselves in prudent reserve while waiting for God to grant us more reliable proofs of His intervention.

IV. THE DISCERNING OF SPIRITS

I Corinthians 12:10. "Beloved, believe not every spirit, but prove the spirits whether they are of God; because many false prophets are gone out into the world" (I John 4:1, 3). Few ages have required this particular gift so much as ours. The spirit of Antichrist is everywhere at work and is increasingly manifest in seduction by error and in denial and revolt, both open and hidden, against God, His Son and His Word. The Devil and his subjects will work wonders even to the point of seducing, if it were possible, God's elect. Already in certain countries, political, national or social movements have created a form of psychosis or collective drive against which many Christians, enlightened though they be, know not how to resist.

In the religious field, the situation is worse, and well can it be said that confusion is greater than ever before, on account of the profusion of sects, of doctrines and of false prophets. We must guard against what we read, for much faulty or corrupt literature is in circulation; beware of what we hear in the world, on the radio, in our families and even in religious circles; watch our very thoughts, for the tempter's voice is unceasingly raised to delude our hearts and consciences. The most serious factor is that everywhere the enemy first appears in an attractive form, disguised as an angel of light (II Cor. 11:14). Since God has placed us in such circumstance, let us ask of Him an ample measure of that gift of discerning of spirits. Let us ardently aspire to it, for without it we run the grave risk of being led astray. God will surely answer our prayer and will guide us into all truth.

V. THE GIFT OF TONGUES

1. There are two kinds of this gift of tongues.

a. The ability to speak one or more foreign languages without having learned them. The sole example we have of this was at Pentecost when the hundred and twenty received the gift of expressing themselves in fifteen different languages and dialects, until then unknown to them (Acts 2:4, 8-11).

b. The gift of talking with God in a form of trance, in a language that is incomprehensible to others and even to our own intelligence, giving to the listener the impression of inarticulate sounds (I Cor. 14:2, 14).

It is of this second gift alone that Paul speaks to the Corinthians, and the following remarks are confined to it:

2. The ability to speak in tongues is useful for personal edification:

"For he that speaketh in a tongue speaketh not unto men, but unto God, for no man understandeth, but in the spirit he speaketh mysteries . . . He that speaketh in a tongue edifieth himself" (I Cor. 14:2, 4).

For this reason this gift, of itself, is of little value to the Church. "If I come unto you speaking with tongues, what shall I profit you, unless I speak to you by way of revelation . . . Unless ye utter by the tongue speech easy to be understood, how shall it be known what is spoken? for ye will be speaking into the air. . . . If then I know not the meaning of the voice, I shall be to him that speaketh a barbarian, and he that speaketh will be a barbarian unto me. . . . How shall he that filleth the place of the unlearned say the Amen at thy giving of thanks, seeing he knoweth not what thou sayest? For thou verily givest thanks well, but the other is not edified. . . . Howbeit, in the church, I had rather speak five words with my understanding, that I might instruct others also, than ten thousand words in a tongue" (I Cor. 14:6, 9, 11, 16-17, 19).

Speaking in tongues is yet more useless when concerned with those who are unconverted: "If therefore, the whole church be assembled together, and all speak with tongues, and there come in men unlearned or unbelieving, will they not say that ye are mad?" (v. 23).

Without a doubt, it is on this account that Paul, in his two lists, mentions the gift of tongues last of all (I Cor. 12:8-10, 28). This is all the more striking in verse 28 where the Apostle seems to establish the degree of importance of each gift: "first apostles, secondly prophets," etc.

3. To be of value to the Church, it must be interpreted.

The aim of spiritual gifts lies not in personal profit but in the edification of the Church. "Wherefore, let him that speaketh in a tongue pray that he may interpret. . . . If any man speaketh in a tongue, let it be by two, or at the most three, and that in turn; and let one interpret; but if there be no interpreter, let him keep silence in the church, and let him speak to himself, and to God" (I Cor. 14:13, 27-28).

4. The gift of tongues is not given to all.

"For to one is given through the Spirit the word of wisdom; and to another the word of knowledge . . . to another divers kinds of tongues. . . . And God hath set some in the church, first apostles . . . then gifts of healings, helps, governments, divers kinds of tongues. Are all apostles? . . . Have all gifts of healings? do all speak with tongues? do all interpret?" (I Cor. 12:8-10, 28-30).

This passage is perfectly clear: all have not the same gifts, but each receives the one chosen for him by God. It is, therefore, altogether wrong to say that any man has not received the Holy Spirit because he cannot speak with tongues.

The Book of Acts fully confirms Paul's words. Throughout its 28 chapters, we can find but three cases of the ability to speak with tongues. For the one hundred and twenty, on the day of Pentecost, and for the Gentiles with Cornelius (Acts 2: 4; 10:44-46), this external sign was required, of necessity, to prove that they had received the Spirit (refer to what has already been said on this point: Part III, Chapter 4). Among all the other believers mentioned in Acts, who were similarly situated as ourselves, we find that only the twelve disciples at Ephesus (19:6-7) spoke with tongues. No Biblical reference gives us the authority to believe that this gift is compulsory for everyone. It is, of course, true that the words of Jesus in Mark 16:17-18, are also quoted: "And these signs shall follow them that believe: in my name shall they cast out devils; they shall speak with new tongues; they shall take up serpents, and if they drink any deadly thing, it shall in no wise hurt them; they shall lay hands on the sick and they shall recover." But if, in accordance with this passage, all were to speak in tongues, all should also cast out devils, take up serpents and be immune to all poisons!

5. The gift of tongues is not a sign of the Spirit's baptism. In the same chapter, Paul declares that not everyone shall speak in tongues, but that *all* are baptized of the Holy Spirit (compare I Cor. 12:10, 30 with v. 13). The point is here clearly settled: in no way are tongues a sign of the Spirit's baptism. If this were otherwise, all would have to receive them since all believers without exception are baptized of the Spirit.

6. Forbid not to speak with tongues, but let all things be done decently and in order.

The whole of chapter 14 of the First Epistle to the Corinthians is devoted to the explanation and proper evaluation of the gift of tongues. In fact, it seems that the Corinthians had allowed some abuse in the exercise of these gifts. Paul gives them precise rules and lays down not a few restrictions since he adds: "Forbid not to speak in tongues. But let all things be done decently and in order. . . . For God is not a God of confusion, but of peace" (I Cor. 14:39-40, 33). Admittedly this constitutes a very negative encouragement; and yet this was necessary for in reaction the Corinthians might have swung to a contrary excess of zeal and forbidden any exercise of such a gift. But who could limit the Spirit's liberty if the rules imposed by Scripture were respected?

The various principles studied above are more than ever of importance in this our age, when the question of speaking with tongues is so frequently met with. Let us, moreover, note that what we read in the Bible has nothing in common with certain manifestations, so prevalent today. When the search for gifts is carried on in a mechanical fashion and that, with this aim in view, hands are laid upon those who are converted, for hours or weeks or months or even longer, while saying to them: "Let yourself go, let your tongue say 'Abba, abba, abba, abba . . .' for as long as you can," for they say that when the Spirit enters into us He cries "Abba," that is to say "Father";

when speech with tongues is accompanied by an excited state of mind, by cries, contortions and among some by a thoroughly unbalanced nervous state; when, as occasionally happens, it is supplemented by "holy laughter" or "spiritual singing" (a sort of inarticulate recitative chanted, as if in a trance, by one person or a whole assembly); in short, when we witness one or other of these phenomena (which occur only too frequently) we are deeply troubled, for we cannot perceive in these the Spirit's gift, and we are again compelled to think of those subtle or debased counterfeits that the enemy is so clever at producing especially in the field of our emotions.

May God give us humility and faithfulness enough to remain open to all that originates from Him and only to that. Then, if in His sovereignty He is pleased to grant us one or another gift of the Spirit, we shall be preserved in Him and certain of glorifying Him.

VI. The Gift of Teaching

The necessary gifts for becoming an evangelist (in the Biblical sense of a herald of the good tidings and a winner of souls), or a pastor (he who feeds the sheep and is concerned with the care of souls), are fairly widespread among us. For this reason, they are not greatly stressed in this study, though it is indeed necessary to ask God to raise up always more of those who are called and prepared by Him and not by man alone. But our religious circles sadly lack "teachers" (I Cor. 12:28; Eph. 4: 11), that is to say, men who teach the Bible and produce a love of sound doctrine. This is easily realized by observing how the love of God's Word and knowledge of elementary truths are lacking even among so-called Christians. There is an urgent need for Biblical teaching to be renewed and given greater depth; this is one of the first conditions for a revival. God, who knows the needs of our age better than we ourselves do, is surely prepared to set up a number of teachers among those who will rise to serve Him. But where are those voluntary helpers who will come forward to support the workers of the present day, often crushed beneath the immensity of the task and calls of ever increasing urgency?

VII. THE GIFT OF HELPS

Certain tasks within the Church seem too humble to require a special gift of the Spirit. And yet it is these more than any other perhaps which call for more than common qualifications. When Paul mentions the gift of helps (I Cor. 12:28), or that of showing mercy (Rom. 12:8), is he not alluding to a ministry such as Tabitha's, for example? From the Acts we learn that she did many good and charitable works, sewing coats and garments for all the widows (9:36, 39). If certain gifts, such as those of apostleship, teaching and government, are on the whole reserved for men, the gift of mercy would appear to fall particularly to the woman's lot. The maternal heart which God has given her can do untold good when filled with the Holy Spirit; there is fine work to be done in connection with the sick, the poor, those in distress, the aged and the lonely. After so many wars and horrors, the world is more than ever filled with souls and bodies requiring succor. Where are those who are prepared to place themselves at God's disposal to carry out among those in need not just social work, but a true ministry of the Spirit?

VIII. THE GIFT OF GOVERNMENTS

The Lord has established a universal priesthood in the Church. All believers are kings and priests (I Peter 2:9; Rev. 1:6) and all have received the anointing from above (I John 2:20, 27). We have already noted elsewhere that it is the Holy Spirit Himself who leads the Church and guides her into all truth.

Despite this, Paul distinctly states that some shall receive the gift of government (I Cor. 12:28). He speaks of a bishop's responsibility in his calling to care for God's Church (I Tim. 3:1, 5). (*Bishop* in Greek means overseer.) Paul also wrote to the Romans: "He that ruleth [let him do it] with diligence" (12:8), and the Epistle to the Hebrews adds, "Obey them that have the rule over you and submit yourselves, for they watch for your souls as they that must give account" (13:17). It was remarked further back that many Christians, if they had their way, would choose the gift of government. (Perhaps it is because everyone wishes to command that anarchy sometimes reigns among us!) But, in truth, in our religious circles the absence of true government imposed by God makes itself felt most cruelly. Those who push to the fore are not always the most spiritual, and they run the risk of allowing themselves to be led more by human wisdom and physical energy than by a gift of the Spirit. Elsewhere, the concept of priesthood is held in such abhorrence that a tendency exists of suppressing any recognized ministry and, above all, the exercise of leadership among brethren. "The Holy Spirit alone shall preside among us," they say. Though, in part, the intention may be sound, do we not hamper the Spirit by prohibiting His endowment of someone with the supernatural gift of government or with leadership allied to humility and based on perfect dependence upon the Lord?

Let us realize that we have a tremendous need of truly Christian statesmen for our churches, our works and our missions. May we pray to God to raise them up and to invest those who already lead with the promised gift of His Spirit.

IX. THE GIFT OF LIBERALITY

It is striking that among the spiritual gifts given to believers, Paul lists that of liberality: "Having gifts differing according to the grace that was given to us . . . he that giveth, let him do it with liberality" (Rom. 12:6-8). All indeed, are called upon to contribute to God's work as the Israelites in former times had, without exception, to give a tithe to the Lord. The apostle, however, here refers to those who have received from God the privilege of having the means and the knowledge to give liberally toward the needs of His cause. He regards them as His special stewards, prudent and faithful servants whom He has set over His people to give them nourishment in due season. Happy are those servants whom the Master, on His return, finds thus employed. Jesus declared that He will set them "over all that he hath" (Matt. 24:45-47). Personally, we have known businessmen wholly consecrated to God, who considered that all their profits, once their personal needs had been met, were for His work. Frequently they gave not only the tenth but a great deal more, and it was amazing to see how God blessed them both spiritually and materially. For such men, the promises contained in II Corinthians 9:6-11 were indeed realized, for the reward to the giver is the ability to give yet more. In short, anyone of our number, even the poorest, can receive such a gift, for if we are faithful in small things, God will entrust us with greater.

Will there not be some reader of this who will feel himself called to the noble task of being a Maecenas (i.e., loyal administrator) in God's cause? The Lord will not fail to grant him by the means of the Spirit the necessary qualities of faith, self-denial, and humility. And, since it is more happy to give than to receive, it is difficult to imagine the great happiness that would accrue to such a minister of the finances of Jesus Christ.

THE EXERCISE OF GIFTS

The gifts of the Spirit are intended not for personal gratification, but for the service of God and of others: "To each is given the manifestation of the Spirit for the common good . . . since you are eager for the manifestations of the Spirit, strive to excel in building up the Church" (I Cor. 12:7; 14:12). "He gave some to be apostles; and some prophets; and some evangelists; and some pastors and teachers, *for the perfecting of the saints,* unto the work of ministering, unto the building up of the Body of Christ" (Eph. 4:11-12).

None has the right to retain for selfish ends what God has given him; indeed this would be the best way to set about losing it, for a light placed under a bushel is inevitably extinguished. On the contrary, Scripture urges us to put it immediately to use: "According as each hath received a gift, ministering it among yourselves as good stewards of the manifold grace of God" (I Peter 4:10). "And having gifts differing . . . whether prophecy, let us prophesy according to the proportion of our faith: or ministry, let us give ourselves to our ministry; or he that teacheth, to his teaching; or he that exhorteth to his exhorting; he that giveth, let him do it with liberality; he that ruleth, with diligence; he that showeth mercy, with cheerfulness" (Rom. 12:6-8). The possession of a gift of the Spirit leads us therefore to joyful service and complete forgetfulness of self. Someone whose attentions are constantly centered on other people, may well in his humility be unconscious of the qualification which he has received; but those who surround him will be aware of it. But one who is above all concerned with himself, placing himself under constant scrutiny, while ceaselessly seeking spiritual gifts for personal ends, will never obtain them.

Since these gifts are granted for the common good, it is in the bosom of the Church apparent that they are exercised. For this reason, Paul having listed and described them, lays down rules for their practice in the assembly of believers (see I Cor. 14:26-40). Let no one, therefore, claim that he can "worship God equally well at home," for if the smallest member withdraws from the Body, the latter is maimed and a vital function is not fulfilled. Under pain of barrenness, every believer according to the direction and understanding given him of God, must bind himself to a spiritual family, in whose circle he will be able to play his part and turn his gifts to good account. Then the talent entrusted to him will bear fruit and achieve its true purpose.

CONCLUSION

Let us summarize in a few words what our attitude should be with regard to spiritual gifts. Paul the apostle indicates its nature to us in these two following injunctions:

1. "Desire earnestly spiritual gifts . . . but desire earnestly the greater gifts" (I Cor. 14:1; 12:31).

We must realize that of ourselves we can do nothing, that without some specific gift of the Spirit, all our human qualifications remain valueless. Let us earnestly ask God to reveal to us the task which He has reserved for us and to grant us that spiritual gift which will enable us to carry it out. If we commit ourselves to Him, we can believe without further delay that we have received the gift and that it will be revealed according to the measure of our needs and obedience. We know, indeed, that all forms of grace are obtained through faith, and that we shall witness the fulfillment of our prayer if we believe that we have received it (Mark 11:24).

But someone may query, "Is not the laying on of hands necessary to receive spiritual gifts?" No, no more than for the reception of the Spirit (see above). In the Book of the Acts we find, for example, that of the three cases where speaking with tongues is mentioned (at Pentecost, at Cornelius' house and at Ephesus [Acts 2; 10; 19]), the first two occur without any laying on of hands. Paul did, indeed, say to Timothy, "Neglect not the gift that is in thee, which was given thee by prophecy with the laying on of the hands of the presbytery" (I Tim. 4: 14). But this passage does not establish a precedent for all men; it merely demonstrates that the laying on of hands is one of the means that God may use to attain this end. The principle chapters on this subject, I Corinthians 12 and 14, do not once mention the laying on of hands as a prerequisite to the reception of a gift and the abiding rule in this case as in all others is that, in the final analysis, every form of grace is obtained through faith.

2. "Stir up the gift of God which is in thee" (II Tim. 1:6).

It may be that God has already given us a gift; our concern, therefore, should no longer be to ask for it, but to stir it into flame. Many Christians bemoan the fact that they are useless, and know not what to do for the Lord. Frequently they follow the example of the servant in the parable, and they too bury their talent in the ground. God, in giving them His Spirit, also granted them a gift; but through unbelief or disobedience, they have allowed this gift to waste away and even to die out for lack of using it. For this reason, God reminds us that we have not received a Spirit of fear, but of strength, love and wisdom. He says to us, as Paul to Timothy, "Neglect not the gift that is in thee" (I Tim. 4:14). If qualified workers are rarely to be found in God's work, the fault can certainly not be attributed to the Lord, but only to those who resist His Spirit. Even as Paul wrote to the Corinthians, "Know ye not that the Holy Spirit is within you?" So could it be said to them, "Know you not that this Spirit has long desired to develop within you a gift to help in the service of the saints, but you have resisted him?" Let us, therefore, stir up our zeal, and renew our full consecration to God; let us obey Him and we shall be amazed to see how He works through us, by virtue of the divine gift which He has placed within us.

CHAPTER 3

THE HOLY SPIRIT AND WITNESS

SPIRITUAL GIFTS are qualifications given to the believer to assist him in his service, and his testimony (witness) is an essential part of the work which these qualifications enable him to achieve.

I. IT IS THE CHARACTERISTIC OF THE SPIRIT TO RENDER WITNESS

"When the Spirit is come . . . he shall bear witness of me . . . for he shall not speak of himself; but what things he shall hear, these shall he speak: and he shall declare unto you the things that are to come. He shall glorify me: for he shall take of mine and shall declare it unto you" (John 15:26; 16:13-14). "And it is the Spirit that beareth witness, because the Spirit is the truth" (I John 5:6).

Since Jesus Christ ascended to Heaven in His risen and glorified body, it is the Spirit's work to witness to Him everywhere. He speaks not of Himself, that is, He does not take the place of the Saviour. On the contrary, He comes to reveal, to glorify and raise up spiritually in us Him who gave Himself for us. Only the Holy Spirit who is one with the Father and the Son knows the things of God and through Him alone can we understand them (I Cor. 2:10-11). Notice that it is to the Son that He bears witness. Indeed, witnessing to the Father can but condemn us, for God, the holy and righteous One, must punish sinners such as we are. But it is by the revelation of His love through Jesus Christ that we are saved. Herein lies the reason for Jesus' declaration that the Spirit will glorify

Him, a declaration bearing no disrespect to the Father because They are one and what belongs to one belongs also to the other (John 16:14-15).

II. BELIEVERS ALSO MUST BEAR WITNESS TO JESUS CHRIST

"And ye also bear witness, because ye have been with me from the beginning" (John 15:27). "If thou shalt confess with thy mouth Jesus as Lord, and shalt believe in thy heart that God raised him from the dead, thou shalt be saved: for with the heart man believeth to righteousness; and with the mouth confession is made unto salvation" (Rom. 10:9-10). God leaves believers on earth that they may introduce others to the salvation which they have found, and Jesus, at the time of His departure from His disciples repeatedly commands them to be everywhere His witnesses (Matt. 28:19; Mark 16:15, etc.). Paul, in the passage quoted above, makes the bearing of witness, together with faith, one of the very conditions of salvation. Faith without works is dead, and a conviction that is never openly avowed probably does not exist; for out of the fullness of the heart the mouth speaks. This is why Jesus said, "Everyone, therefore, who shall confess me before men, will I also confess before my Father which is in heaven. But whosoever shall deny me before men, him will I also deny before my father which is in heaven" (Matt. 10:32-33).

Are we obedient to such an explicit commandment, or do we retire within ourselves on account of frailty and apprehensiveness? If the latter be the case we shall be bereft of any excuse, for the Lord who gives us this commandment also gives us the strength to carry it out.

III. IT IS THROUGH THE POWER OF THE SPIRIT THAT WE ARE ABLE TO BEAR WITNESS

Jesus knew His disciples' frailty and their individual inability to proclaim His message. Therefore He said to them, "Ye are witnesses of these things. *And behold* I send forth the promise of my Father upon you: but tarry ye in the city, until ye be clothed with power from on high" (Luke 24:48-49). To which He added, "Ye shall receive power when the Holy Ghost is come upon you: and ye shall be my witnesses both in Jerusalem and in all Judea and Samaria, and unto the uttermost part of the earth" (Acts 1:8).

It would have been completely useless had the disciples been left to themselves to go forth and bear witness, whereas after they had received the Spirit, given for this very purpose, the point at issue was no longer their frailty but His power. Thus we read that the disciples, armed with invincible courage, carried victory after victory in the name of Jesus Christ. Thus they were able to say wherever they found themselves, "We are witnesses of these things; and so is the Holy Ghost whom God hath given to them that obey Him" (Acts 5:32). When Stephen disputed with his opponents "they were not able to withstand the wisdom and the Spirit by which he spake" (Acts 6:10).

Paul was the great apostle to the Gentiles because his preaching and his speech "were not in persuasive words of wisdom but in demonstration of the Spirit and of power," and because his Gospel "came . . . not in word only, but also in power and in the Holy Ghost and in much assurance" (I Cor. 2:4; I Thess. 1:5).

If we could but affirm these same things today, how much more fruitful our witness would be! May God grant that we become witnesses and preachers who go armed not with the carnal weapons of wisdom and human reasoning but, relying only on the power of the Spirit, with the invincible sword, the Word of God (Eph. 6:17). Wherefore, let us cease from dwelling on our own inadequacy and allow the Spirit to act and speak through us. He will give us love for souls, wisdom from above, and all-conquering power. Then shall we not stand confused on that day when Jesus Christ must acknowledge us before His Father.

CHAPTER 4

THE HOLY SPIRIT AND PRAYER

THE SPIRIT ALSO HELPETH OUR INFIRMITY: for we know not how to pray as we ought; but the Spirit himself maketh intercession for us with groanings which cannot be uttered; and he that searcheth the hearts knoweth what is the mind of the Spirit, because he maketh intercession for the saints according to the will of God" (Rom. 8:26-27). By our very nature we know not how to pray and have need of this supernatural aid for many reasons.

I. OUR PRAYERS ARE SELFISH

They always lead back to ourselves, and it is only the Spirit who teaches us to pray for the kingdom of God and for others. In this context it is worth noting that the first three out of six requests in the Lord's prayer center round God: His name, His kingdom and His will (Matt. 6:9-10). The passage from Romans 8, quoted above, speaks twice of the Spirit interceding. When we devote ourselves in all sincerity to prayer it is without doubt the Spirit who inspires us. Through earnest prayer He makes of us, perpetual beggars that we are, fellow workers with God.

II. OUR PRAYERS LACK INSIGHT

Scripture promises that "if we ask anything according to his will he heareth us" (I John 5:14). But, at times, our great difficulty is to know precisely what the will of God is, to understand how to frame our prayer. Moreover, how frequently our requests are stillborn because they are counter to the Lord's plan. Indeed, we know not what to ask for in our prayer, yet God knows our weakness and comes to our aid through His Spirit, who leads us into all truth, and He Himself inspires our requests in accordance with the "will of God"; thus can they be answered. How altered and confident our life of prayer then becomes!

III. OUR PRAYERS ARE COLD

We pray too often as a duty, giving lip service. Our requests lack fervor because our hearts and minds remain indifferent when faced with the seriousness of sin, the loss of souls, and God's interests. Paul, therefore, says to the Romans: "I beseech you . . . by the love of the Spirit, that ye strive together with me in your prayers to God for me" (15:30). The word *strive* is here used with intentional force. It implies agonizing, wrestling to the point of death in prayer. How can we pray with such fervor unless the love of the Spirit fills our hearts? Elsewhere this same Spirit is called the Spirit of supplication (Zech. 12:10), and we know that He intercedes for us with longings which cannot be expressed in words (Rom. 8:26). The great men of the Old Testament, under the Spirit's impulse, strove in prayer and of these, what great examples we have in Ezra (9:3; 10:6) and in Daniel (9:3-23; 10:2-3)!

IV. OUR PRAYERS ARE INTERMITTENT

It may happen that we do pray and with great earnestness, but we find it difficult to persevere in steadfast prayer. Here again, it is only the Spirit who can come to our aid. If we yield ourselves to Him, He revives and feeds continually the flame within us; He opens a ceaseless source of living water, springing up to life eternal. Paul expresses it in this manner: "With all prayer and supplication, praying at all seasons *in the Spirit*, and watching thereunto in all perseverance and supplication for all the saints, and on my behalf" (Eph. 6:18-19). May we pray steadfastly in the Spirit, and God who is not an unjust judge will answer us.

V. OUR PRAYERS LACK POWER AND FAITH

Clearly, if our prayers are selfish, cold and irregular or lacking in understanding, they cannot be powerful. But frequently our requests also remain empty because they are not supported by faith. Yet, without faith, it is impossible to be pleasing to God (Heb. 11:6) and if we doubt, we need not imagine we shall receive aught at His hand (James 1:6-7). Who else, therefore, can supply our wants if it be not the Spirit of faith and power? (II Cor. 4:13; Eph. 3:20).

CONCLUSION

In the light of such knowledge, we must not content ourselves with repeating the disciples' demand: "Lord, teach us to pray." We have received the One who is the source of all true prayer. He pleads within us, while Christ mediates between us and God (Rom. 8:34). How strongly supported are our requests! May we allow the Lord to inspire our life of prayer and He will transform it. What tranquillity and strength result from such a communion wherein the Spirit and the believer share the same desire! It is the fulfillment of what is expressed thus in one passage of Scripture: "The Spirit and the bride say Come" (Rev. 22:17). When man's prayer is in harmony with God's will, the answer and victory are near at hand.

"But ye, beloved, building up yourselves in your most holy faith, praying in the Holy Spirit, keep yourselves in the love of God, looking for the mercy of our Lord Jesus Christ unto eternal life" (Jude 20, 21).

CHAPTER 5

THE HOLY SPIRIT AND WORSHIP

THE HIGHEST FORM of service is worship. The glimpse which the Book of Revelation affords us of the redeemed in Heaven reveals them in an attitude of worship, praising both the Lamb and Him who sits on the throne (Rev. 4:9-11; 5:8-14, etc.).

Jesus said: "God is a Spirit, and they that worship him must worship him in Spirit and in truth" (John 4:24). No doubt He did imply by this that our worship should neither be material nor attached, as the Samaritans believed, to one place or another, to rites, ceremonies or special vestments. Yet, His words have a deeper significance. Man is earthly and carnal; therefore, how can he have a vision of God, the Holy and Infinite; how can he come to know Him sufficiently well to approach Him, to meditate on Him, to praise, revere and adore Him? Scripture indeed gives man a perfect revelation, but who will transfer it from the written page to his heart and soul? It is the Spirit who will achieve this, who will bridge the gap and introduce into him the very presence of God the Saviour; then will He awaken, love, awe, thankfulness, obedience, praise, in short, that true worship of a God so perfect and good.

Thus Paul could state that "we are the circumcision, who worship by the Spirit of God" (Phil. 3:3). In past days under the Old Covenant, men were constrained to serve God by the law and fear of punishment. "But now," says Paul, "we have been discharged from the law ... so that we serve in newness of the Spirit and not in oldness of the letter" (Rom. 7:6). It is indeed through an inward strength and presence acting in us that our souls are lifted up to God with joy. What a privilege is ours!

We can make another comparison with the Old Covenant. In levitical worship, oil was the symbol of the Holy Spirit. The priests were prepared for the service of the Lord by being anointed and sprinkled with oil according to Moses' instructions: "Thou shalt anoint Aaron and his sons and sanctify them that they may minister to me in the priest's office" (Exod. 30:30). Then, when they entered the sanctuary, they performed their ministry by the light of the holy oil which burned continually in the candlesticks (Exod. 27:20). Even so today, it is through the Spirit that we can offer to God worship that is pleasing to Him. The Spirit sanctifies and cleanses us from the defilement which separates us from the Lord; then, He reveals to us the truths of divine perfection, and guides us step by step in the spiritual worship which we should offer, controlling our feelings, inspiring our thoughts and creating in us both the desire and the ability to act according to His will.

This worship, inspired by the Spirit, is offered to both the Father and the Son. It is through Jesus Christ and His work that "we both have our access in one Spirit unto the Father" (Eph. 2:18). Moreover, "no man can say Jesus Christ is Lord, but in the Holy Spirit" (I Cor. 12:3). "Hereby know ye the Spirit of God: every Spirit which confesseth that Jesus Christ is come in the flesh, is of God" (I John 4:2). This is only natural since the Spirit's role is to glorify Jesus, and the Father and the Son are one.

What of our worship? Is it offered to a God of our own conception or to the God of the Bible, Father, Son and Holy Spirit? Even if we know Him, is our worship still carnal and selfish or purified by the Spirit? If we are true worshipers we with unveiled faces can gaze, as it were in a mirror, upon the glory of the Lord and be transformed into the same image from glory to glory even as from the Lord the Spirit (II Cor. 3:18).

PART V

THE WORK OF THE SPIRIT
IN THE FUTURE

CHAPTER 1

THE HOLY SPIRIT AND ISRAEL

I. THE CONVERSION OF THE JEWS

IN STUDYING THE OLD TESTAMENT we have seen (page 34) in what terms God promised His people that by virtue of a new covenant He would shortly place His Spirit forever in the hearts of all believers. Yet Israel has rejected both this covenant and the Mediator who offered it to them; will they therefore, be forever bereft of the grace of the Spirit? No, indeed, Scripture declares in a number of passages that in the last days Israel will foregather again in Palestine, that the Spirit will be poured out upon them and that the nation will recognize Jesus Christ as the Messiah.

Isaiah proclaimed that Palestine would be deserted and arid "until the Spirit be poured upon us from on high and the wilderness become a fruitful field. . . . No one of these shall be missing. . . . His Spirit hath gathered them [the children of Israel in Palestine] . . . for I will pour water upon him that is thirsty, and streams on the dry ground. I will pour my Spirit upon thy seed, and my blessing upon thine offspring. . . . This is my covenant with them, saith the Lord: My Spirit that is upon thee, and my words which I have put in thy mouth, shall not depart out of thy mouth nor out of the mouth of thy seed, nor out of the mouth of thy seed's seed, saith the Lord, from henceforth and forever" (Isa. 32:15; 34:16; 44:3; 59:21).

Ezekiel, having announced the universal promise of the gift of the Spirit, which has already been fulfilled for us (36:26-27), tells of the vision he saw of Israel in terms of dry bones.

213

The Lord said to him: "Son of man, these bones are the whole house of Israel: behold they say, Our bones are dried up, and our hope is lost: we are clean cut off. Therefore prophesy and say unto them . . . I will put my Spirit in you and ye shall live, and I will place you in your own land, and ye shall know that I the Lord have spoken it, and performed it, saith the Lord" (Ezek. 37:11-14). These passages quoted above clearly indicate that the outpouring of the Spirit on the Jewish people will take place when God leads them back to Palestine and causes the land to flourish as in former times. It would appear that this moment is no longer so remote. Zechariah also foretells that Israel, gathered together from the distant corners of the earth (8:1-8; 10:6-10) will be attacked in Jerusalem by all nations (12:3, 9). "And I will pour upon the house of David, and upon the inhabitants of Jerusalem, the Spirit of grace and supplication; and they shall look unto me whom they have pierced; and they shall mourn for him as one mourneth for his only son" (Zech. 12:10).

Then the Spirit will do for the Jews what He has done for the world: He will convict them of sin, for their disbelief in Jesus Christ. They will humble themselves and repent and the outcome of this great awakening will be their conversion to the Saviour. Paul himself, alluded to these coming events when he wrote, "A hardening in part hath befallen Israel, until the fullness of the Gentiles be come in [i.e., the total number of Gentiles who are to belong to the Church]; and so all Israel shall be saved; even as it is written,

"There shall come out of Zion the Deliverer;
He shall turn away ungodliness from Jacob:
And this is my covenant unto them,
When I shall take away their sins" (Rom. 11:25-27).

The conversion of the Jews under the Spirit's influence will be the signal for the coming of the greatest blessings on humanity according to the promise that the receiving of them will be "life from the dead" (Rom. 11:15). For then, in His glory, shall appear Jesus Christ the great Conqueror who shall judge the world and establish over all the earth His reign of justice and peace (Zech. 14:5). When thinking of such bless-ings, how great is our desire to hasten their coming! We see already that the dry bones are being brought together, and filled with quickened hope, we cry, "Come from the four winds, O Breath, and breathe upon these slain that they may live" (Ezek. 37:9). Blessed is He who proclaims, "Say unto the cities of Judah, Behold your God! Behold the Lord God will come as a mighty one, and his arm shall rule for him; behold his reward is with him and his recompense before him. He shall feed his flock as a shepherd and he shall gather the lambs in his arm and carry them in his bosom, and shall gently lead those that give suck" (Isa. 40:9-11).

Lord Jesus, come soon to pour Thy Spirit upon Thy people Israel!

II. WILL THE SPIRIT REMAIN ON EARTH DURING THE GREAT TRIBULATION?

A certain number of commentators on prophecy—but by no means all—have questioned on the basis of a supposition of their own whether the Holy Spirit will not be taken away from the earth, together with the Church, before the great tribulation, and therefore before the conversion of Israel. To support this opinion, the following text is quoted: "It [i.e., the return of Christ (v. 2)] will not be, except the falling away come first and the man of sin be revealed, and the son of perdition [i.e., Antichrist]. . . . For the mystery of lawlessness doth already work: only there is one that restraineth now, until he be taken out of the way. And then shall be revealed the lawless one, whom the Lord Jesus shall slay with the breath of his mouth, and bring to nought by the manifestation of his coming" (II Thess. 2:3-8). Who is the *One* whose presence prevents the appearing of Antichrist? It is claimed that this cannot be any other than the Holy Spirit, whose temple here

below is the faithful Church (Eph. 2:21, 22); and who therefore will be drawn up into the heavens together with the latter.
Since Antichrist must reign quite openly during three and a
half years (Rev. 13:5, a period known as that of the Great
Tribulation), the Spirit's departure must take place before this
time of tribulation.

It is not our intention in this context to solve the question
fully, confining ourselves rather to noting certain points arising
from it. If it is true that the Church, the temple of the Spirit
and the salt of the earth, is taken up into the heavens at a
given moment and that her departure is marked by a greatly
increased spiritual decline, it remains none the less true that the
Spirit will continue to act among men though perhaps in a
different fashion.

1. The Spirit will be poured out upon Israel (as we have
just seen) during the Great Tribulation, i.e., when Antichrist,
having broken his pact with the Jews, will seek to exterminate
them during the three and a half years of his undisputed rule
(Dan. 9:27; Zech. 12:9-10).

2. During the time marked by the departure of the Church
and the coming of Christ to judge, men from all nations will
be converted to the Gospel. Indeed, at the start of the Millennium those who, during the Great Tribulation, will have been
put to death for not worshiping Antichrist, will be raised up
(Rev. 20:4). They were not believers when the Church was
withdrawn, else they would have been taken also, but confessed belief later. How could they have done this without the
Holy Spirit? He alone brings conviction and regeneration;
those who have not the Spirit do not belong to Christ (Rom.
8:9), while those who believe become forthwith His temple.
No passage in Scripture gives us ground for believing that
those who are converted during the Great Tribulation will be
able to dispense with the ministration of the Spirit who alone
conveys salvation to us.

3. A remarkable verse in Isaiah states: "When the enemy

shall come in like a flood, the Spirit of the Lord shall lift up a standard against him. And the Redeemer shall come to Zion and unto them that turn from transgression in Jacob" (59:19-20). It would seem that reference is clearly made here to the last days. Moreover when shall the enemy most closely resemble the rushing of a flood if it be not when the rising tide of Antichrist will threaten to overwhelm all? This text warrants the belief that the Spirit will, to the very end, contribute to Christ's triumph over the forces of evil.

In conclusion we can say that the withdrawal of the Church, whatever its consequences may be, will not entail a complete cessation of the Spirit's work here below. Furthermore, we do not in any way wish to dogmatize on this matter in the foregoing remarks. If any reader is interested in this question, he is advised to make a personal study of *all* the passages connected with this matter.

CHAPTER 2

THE HOLY SPIRIT AND THE RESURRECTION

THERE ARE FEW TEXTS which allude to the resurrection through the Spirit, yet their message is crystal clear.

"If the Spirit of him that raised up Jesus from the dead dwelleth in you, he that raised up Christ Jesus from the dead shall quicken also your mortal bodies through his Spirit that dwelleth in you" (Rom. 8:11). "For we through the Spirit by faith wait for the hope of righteousness . . . He that soweth unto the Spirit shall of the Spirit reap eternal life" (Gal. 5:5; 6:8). God raised Christ from the grave by His Spirit through whom our mortal bodies also shall be raised. Jesus implied this when He said, "It is the Spirit that quickeneth; the flesh profiteth nothing" (John 6:63). This He said after He had been talking to the Jews of the twofold manner in which He gave men life, "This is the will of my Father, that everyone that beholdeth the Son, and believeth on him, should have eternal life; and I will raise him up at the last day" (John 6:40). The significance of this is that:

1. He shall give life immediately to the soul of every believer.

2. He will raise his body on the last day.

Since it is through the Spirit that the soul is regenerated (John 3:5), it is scarcely surprising that the same Spirit should bring about the resurrection of the body; besides, the first miracle is far more extraordinary than the latter.

Let us note, furthermore, that with the resurrection, as in the creation and every other divine intervention, we find the combined action of Father, Son and Spirit, since it is attributed

218

to all these at the same time (re-read Rom. 8:11 and John 6:40). It cannot be otherwise, as the three Persons of the Trinity are One. In another passage previously alluded to, we find a wonderful illustration of the resurrection through the Spirit (Ezek. 37:1-14). Though its primary application is to Israel, it also serves to illustrate the resurrection of all those who will have believed. God carried the prophet in the spirit to a valley filled with numberless dry bones, and said to him: "Son of man, can these bones live? And I answered, O Lord God, thou knowest. Again he said unto me, Prophesy over these bones and say unto them, O ye dry bones, hear the word of the Lord. Thus saith the Lord God. . . . Behold I will cause breath to enter into you and ye shall live. . . . So I prophesied and he commanded me, and the breath came unto them and they lived, and stood upon their feet, an exceeding great army."

The day is near when the Spirit of God will breathe from the four winds over the whole earth. Those who have died in Christ will rise first, then those who are still alive at the moment of the Lord's coming shall be changed and we shall all rise to meet Him, to live eternally with Him in glory (I Thess. 4:16-17). Are we certain of being among those whom the Spirit will raise to life and not to judgment?

CHAPTER 3

THE HOLY SPIRIT IN ETERNITY

IT IS CLEAR that the Spirit's activity, which is eternal, will not be concluded when the present world reaches its final destruction. He is an integral part of the Divine Being and the Father, the Son and the Holy Spirit who have ceaselessly acted in concert in the past will so continue in eternity. Though giving us no details, Scripture conveys to us an understanding of the nature of the Spirit's work on behalf of the redeemed in the hereafter.

The greatest spiritual grace of which we can lay hold in this present time represents but a foretaste of that which awaits us in glory. Paul states that we have only received the first fruits, or the pledge of the Spirit: "Ourselves also, which have the first fruits of the Spirit . . . groan within ourselves, waiting for our adoption, to wit, the redemption of our body . . . God . . . also sealed us and gave us the earnest of the Spirit in our hearts . . . For verily in this [earthly house] we groan, longing to be clothed upon with our habitation which is from heaven . . . Now he that wrought for us that very thing is God, who gave unto us the earnest of the Spirit" (Rom. 8:23; II Cor. 1:22; 5:2-5). From these passages we learn that when we enter into eternity we shall receive an infinitely greater measure of the Spirit than is possible in the present time even though filled by Him to the extent of our feeble capacity.

Scripture in truth teaches us that "we shall be like him [the Lord]; for we shall see him even as he is" (I John 3:2). All sin and unbelief will disappear and nothing will hinder the Spirit, who will have fashioned us in the image of Jesus Christ

(Rom. 8:29; II Cor. 3:18), from taking full possession of our being. Then will the promise, found in the Epistle to the Ephesians, be fully realized: having attained unto "the measure of the stature of the fullness of Christ," we shall be filled by the Spirit "unto the fullness of God" (Eph. 4:13; 3:16-19). We have already noted that here below the Spirit has, with the Father and the Son, His place in us. So it will be in Heaven too, but to an infinitely greater degree of perfection. In a manner most absolute, Christ will become the One "that filleth all in all"; He will be "all and in all" (Eph. 1:23; Col. 3:11), and the Father Himself, when all things have been subjected unto Him, will become "all in all" (I Cor. 15:28).

The human tongue is powerless to express the glory, the holiness, the joy and power which will then be the portion of the redeemed. Eternity will be too short to worship, praise and serve the Author of our salvation, the thrice-holy God, Father, Son and Holy Spirit. And even now, reflecting on these things, we rejoice with joy unspeakable and glorious.

Let us not, however, be under any illusion. That God will one day be all in all does not at all imply, as some would claim, that all men and every creature will be saved, the Devil included! It is dangerous to divorce a Biblical statement from its context. Prior to stating that Christ "is all and in all," Paul announces that the wrath of God shall descend on the sons of disobedience who continue in sin; it is only to those who have "put off the old man with his doings, and have put on the new man" [the Lord's presence in them through the Spirit] that Christ is all in all, regardless of racial or social discrimination (Col. 3:5-11). The word *all* therefore applies only to believers. The passage from which we learn that finally God will be "all in all" bears the same significance (I Cor. 15:28). In this same chapter Paul solemnly states that without faith in Christ and in His bodily resurrection we would yet be lost in sin, the most miserable of men (vv. 18-19), and that flesh and blood cannot inherit the Kingdom of God, neither corruption inherit incorruption (v. 50). Let us bear in mind that the Epistles were written for those who believe and not for those that stand without. This is again clearly underlined in verses 22 and 23 of the same chapter: "For as in Adam all die, so in Christ shall all be made alive." Were we to stop there we might well ask if all men, even those who died in unbelief, shall be made alive in Christ. However verse 23 specifies, "But each in his own order; Christ the first fruits; then *they that are Christ's,* at his coming." The phrase "all be made alive" applies therefore only to those who belong to Christ.

This agrees in every respect with the teaching of Christ and His apostles regarding the unforgivable sin against the Spirit (Mark 3:24), everlasting damnation (Matt. 25:41, 46), and the statement that after death will come judgment (Heb. 9: 27). Yes, indeed, God through the Spirit will be all in all, after placing all His enemies in subjection under His feet, but only in all who while here below have received the pledge (of the Spirit). They have received a token of the pact made in faith between God and themselves, therefore perfect and eternal salvation is reserved for them in heaven. Are we indeed one of this number? Let us make certain that our hearts are not hardened and that we are ready to enter the world of the Spirit where, forever, we shall see God face to face.

CONCLUSION

Has not Jesus Christ's promise been perfectly fulfilled? In reality the Spirit has not spoken to us of Himself but, before our eyes He has glorified the Saviour. He has convicted us of the sin of having rejected Christ and has given us faith in Him; He has brought His life to us and through baptism He has made us, who have believed, members of His body; He has led us to the point of adoption and to the certainty of salvation through Jesus Christ; He lives in us together with Him who is our wisdom, our righteousness, our sanctification and our redemption; He also desires to bestow upon us His fullness and transform us into His image; He will soon convert Israel to the Messiah; then, in glory He will at last perfect our likeness to the Lord, and God who is Spirit will become all in all.

Now that we have reached the conclusion of this study, do we not feel impelled to worship and praise the Author of a salvation so perfect? Let us bear in mind, however, that our worship will be in vain if we hinder the Spirit's work in ourselves. We would be both insane and guilty if, with the insight that we have received, we omitted to seek the Spirit's aid in all things, or consciously resisted Him. May God give us grace to yield ourselves unreservedly and joyfully into His hands that through the Spirit He may accomplish in us, to the glory of the Son, all that is pleasing to Him.

"Now unto him that is able to do exceeding abundantly above all that we ask or think, according to the power that worketh in us, unto him be the glory in the church and in Christ Jesus unto all generations for ever and ever. Amen" (Eph. 3:20-21).

Moody Press, a ministry of the Moody Bible Institute, is designed for education, evangelization and edification. If we may assist you in knowing more about Christ and the Christian life, please write us without obligation to: Moody Press, c/o MLM, Chicago, Illinois 60610.